THE IDEA OF MUSIC

Schoenberg and others

THE IDEA OF MUSIC
Schoenberg and others

by

PETER FRANKLIN

MACMILLAN

© Peter Franklin   1985

First published 1985

Published by
THE MACMILLAN PRESS LTD
Houndmills, Basingstoke, Hampshire RG21 2XS
and London
Companies and representatives
throughout the world

Typeset in 11pt Plantin
and printed in Malta by
Interprint Ltd

ISBN 0 333 40027 5 (hardback)
      0 333 40028 3 (paperback)

British Library Cataloguing in Publication Data
Franklin, Peter
The idea of music: Schoenberg and others.
1. Music—Philosophy and aesthetics   2. Music
—History and criticism—20th century
I. Title
780′.1   ML3800

ISBN 0-333-40027-5
ISBN 0-333-40028-3 Pbk

Contents

Acknowledgements   vii

Introduction   xi

1. Music, the Will and Ideas   1
2. Strauss's Transfiguration   19
3. The Problem of *Doctor Faustus*   35
4. Adorno's *Philosophy of Modern Music*   55
5. An Essay by Schoenberg   77
6. Chaos, the Machine or the Mystic Word   91
7. *Palestrina* and the Dangerous Futurists   117
8. Schreker's Decline   139

Conclusion   161

Notes   169

Index   183

Acknowledgements

I should like to thank the following publishers for permission to quote from works whose copyright they hold: Dover Publications Inc., New York (for Schopenhauer, *The World as Will and Representation*), Martin Secker and Warburg Ltd, London (for Thomas Mann, *Doctor Faustus*), Continuum Publishing Co., New York (for Adorno, *Philosophy of Modern Music*) and Faber and Faber, London (for Schoenberg, *Style and Idea*). I am also grateful to G. Schirmer, New York, for permission to include here a revised version of '*Palestrina* and the Dangerous Futurists', which originally appeared in the *Musical Quarterly*, Fall 1984.

My thanks are also warmly offered to Jannet King, for her hard work and encouragement, to Chris Hogan, for counting and checking, and to Keith Sherlock, for hearing and reading it all so many times. A particular debt of gratitude is owed to Christopher Hailey, of Bethany, Connecticut, whose extensive knowledge of the music of Franz Schreker, and much else, has so readily been brought to bear on so many of my questions.

All true, all original music is a swan's song. –
Perhaps even our latest music, notwithstanding
its predominance and ambition, has but a brief
span of time before it; for it originated out of a
civilisation whose basis is rapidly sinking, – a
forthwith sunken *civilization.*

Nietzsche: 'Nietzsche contra Wagner'[1]

Introduction

If one's aim is to question established ideas about a period of history, it is as well not to begin dogmatically. The proper course must be to piece together a case with reference to specific problematic areas, hoping at least to generate debate from which more significant conclusions might arise. Nowhere is such a course of action more advisable than in the history of an art-form like music – and particularly twentieth-century European music. The sheer mass of available works, from a large number of national traditions, defies the cataloguer and confounds the historian, whose business is traditionally that of making sense of the data, of selecting from it and arranging it into a coherent picture of change and renewal, progress and decline.

The problem about the recent history of an art-form is not so much that of too great a proximity. Rather than affording greater objectivity, the distancing of time merely allows us to forget those pieces that do not fit into the picture. It also permits us more easily to evade the uncomfortable truth that the very historical picture whose currency we endorse started life as a highly selective arrangement of facts, whose initial rationale may well have been primarily critical or didactic.

Serious writing on music tends nowadays to fight

shy of criticism, preferring to don the white coat of the 'analyst' and concern itself with notes rather than possibly irrelevant ideas about them. But what notes, and why? Since Alan Walker and Hans Keller demonstrated that the once critically frowned-upon symphonies of Tchaikovsky were 'in fact' remarkably well-organized compositions, analysis has acted as a kind of covert criticism, or rather has attempted to replace critical values with the demonstrable facts of integrated and economical organization (allowing, perhaps, of an attractive schematic précis in the Schenkerian manner). But anything can be analysed and the historian's problem is in no wise solved.

The crucial question is: does an acceptance of the necessarily subjective basis of traditional art history, with its selective rather than statistical tendency, negate its value altogether? It depends, of course, on what we want from it. The kind of history that apprises school-children of the fact that Beethoven wrote nine symphonies and came before Brahms, who wrote four, presents few problems. The kind of history that admits the question as to why we concentrate on Beethoven rather than Hummel presents more problems, in that values are brought into play which depend upon critical as much as analytic justification; and to suscribe openly to critical values is to stand ideologically naked in a way that might well merit embarrassment if we could see ourselves from all directions at once.

It is, nevertheless, precisely the lack of a really fruitful critical debate that has allowed the 'history of twentieth-century music' to solidify so quickly into the form of a mythic picture that depends upon the radical propaganda on behalf of a small, if remarkable, coterie of problematic pioneers of the early twentieth century, whose idiosyncratic notions about artistic progress significantly sundered them from what in merely statistical terms would have to be considered the mainstream. Since this propaganda, be it by specific composers speaking on their own behalf or by ardent pupils and adherents, produced a more committed body of literature to which the scholarly historian might refer than the 'reactionary' mainstream, the seeds were early sown of a mythic history whose overriding justification seemed to be that insight of *critical* history that in the past it was the misunderstood and isolated innovator who often enough turned out to be the real torchbearer.

In spite of Boulez, Stravinsky and others, I am inclined to see the roots of the problem, of problematic 'modern music' indeed, precisely in the Austro-German tradition that so effectively dominated Western art-music in the nineteenth century. It is its achievements, its death-throes and attempts at self-renewal that I am concerned to re-examine here in a critical light. I must state at once that it is not my purpose merely to disparage or to dislodge Schoenberg, Berg and Webern from their richly deserved positions as problematic patrons of Modern Music. What it is my purpose to suggest is that they have received an acclaim that dangerously has come almost to deny the possibility of critical scrutiny. This is the inevitable result of the propaganda basis of their reputation, which has had the curious effect of award-

ing other, equally important composers (if for
different reasons) within the same tradition merely
ancillary roles to the highly esoteric achievements of
the Second Viennese School. Thus Mahler may
become a 'precursor' of expressionism, Strauss a
conservative regressive after *Elektra,* while other
figures of great importance in their day have been
summarily dispensed with simply because they do not
fit into the picture that centres upon Schoenberg and
his pupils.

It is out of concern at this apparent over-simplific-
ation, at the conspicuous lack of what F. R. Leavis
would have called 'collaborative critical debate' in this
area, that the essays in this volume seek to experiment
with alternative critical approaches in a historical
perspective, initially to establish a case for Mahler as a
landmark rather than a bridge, and for Strauss as a
'survivor' from whom much may yet be learned.
Attention is latterly turned to two figures whose names
tend now to mean comparatively little, for reasons
indicated above. The central group of studies seeks
conversely to consider in a critical light the creative
phenomena that were to forge the image of progressive
music whose problematic aspect has bedevilled
audiences, critics and historians alike for half a
century.

I must return, however, to my opening rejection of
critical dogma. The aim of these essays is to provoke
thought rather than to destroy reputations. Their
central theme is specifically that, in these analytical
times, we ignore the conceptual content and implications of twentieth-century music at our peril – content

and implications which depend upon the late nineteenth century's creation, for better or worse, of a
music that functioned as an expressive image of the
human mind in its most modern aspect. The relative
freedom or stylistic restriction of this music came to
depend more upon composers' conscious or unconscious attitudes towards such age-old problems as
the Freedom of the Will or man's capacity for
perceiving Truth than the solution of purely musical
problems (in the terminology of a more traditional
aesthetic approach). The outcome of our consideration
of composers' ideas, alongside the art that these ideas
conditioned, might well be a renewed respect for both
progressive and conservative branches of serious
modern music. Both are perhaps equally relevant to a
consideration of the profound human troubles of our
century that might otherwise seem so far to transcend
the fussing of a handful of otherworldly musicians
about what they might or might not permit themselves
to do in their art.

ONE

Music, the Will and Ideas

When Bruno Walter first came to know Mahler during
the years 1894–6, he found the composer to be much
influenced by a writer – not of musical theory or
history, but of philosophy. The philosopher was
Schopenhauer, a complete edition of whose works
Walter once received as a Christmas present from
Mahler.[1] It is a fact that need cause us little initial
surprise. Highly literate and literary a musician as he
was, Mahler, who had in his youth been an almost
fanatically devoted Wagnerian, would naturally have
found his way sooner or later to those works which
Wagner described as having come to him "like a gift
from heaven"[2] in 1854. Many aspects of the programmatic basis of the Third Symphony – largely composed during the summers of 1895 and 1896 – suggest
that Mahler's volumes of Schopenhauer were perhaps
never far from hand during those years. Some of his
recorded comments support this view, and the sections
dealing with music seem to have held particular significance for him. A footnote by Alma Mahler to a letter
of 1892 from her husband to Arnold Berliner (to

I

whom Mahler had given a copy of Wagner's Schopenhauer-inspired *Beethoven*) attests to his belief that

> on the *essence* of music, apart from Wagner in *Beethoven*, only Schopenhauer in *The World as Will and Representation* had anything valuable to say. Berliner once heard him describe the section in *The World as Will and Representation* as the most profound that, to his knowledge, was ever likely to be written on the subject.[3]

Precisely how far Mahler's sympathy with the philosopher extended beyond the sections on music is more difficult to assess than Bruno Walter's account might indicate, however. Part of a conversation with Mahler, which Walter records earlier in his little book on the composer, is relevant here. He is described as having uttered the following "with deep emotion, while his troubled look gave evidence of the convulsion of his soul from which he had just freed himself":

> How dark is the foundation upon which our life rests.... Whence do we come, whither does our road take us? Have I really willed this life, as Schopenhauer thinks, before I even was conceived? Why am I made to feel that I am free while yet I am constrained within my character as in a prison? What is the object of toil and sorrow? How am I to understand the cruelty and malice in the creations of a kind God? Will the meaning of life be finally revealed by death?[4]

On the evidence of this one might rather see Mahler – the Faustian metaphysician recalled by Ferdinand Pfohl as "one who had questioned God and accordingly been cast out of the Light and into the Darkness"[5] – as struggling beneath the *shadow* of Schopenhauer; struggling to find an alternative to the gloomy picture of the world that Wagner's philosopher had so convincingly painted in *The World as Will and Representation* (first published in 1818).

$$\star \quad \star \quad \star$$

Regarding himself as heir and successor to Kant, Schopenhauer accepted the essentials of that philosopher's understanding of the world as in reality 'known' to us only in terms of the interconnecting pictures, or 'representations', of it which the brain conveniently creates from the data supplied to it by the senses. Only thus, as it were bumping into objects in the dark, do we approach the 'Thing-in-Itself', which – since we may never leave the island of human consciousness, never remove the tinted spectacles with which it is by nature furnished – we can in no way know 'as it is'. Here, however, Schopenhauer had more to say: adding to Kant's world of 'representation' an in-itself world of Will.[6]

Schopenhauer remarked that there is one Thing-in-Itself which we do indeed know from within, as something other than mere 'representation': the human being, *ourself* – the self which we also know as the embodiment of 'Will'. With daemonic inspiration, clearly native to the century of Goethe's *Faust*, the

3

century that was to give birth to Freud, Schopenhauer went on to question whether we could have any possible grounds to consider that this duality of outer (representation – the physical 'object') and inner nature (Will), which we perceive in ourselves, did not hold for all representable objects; for the entire physical world. This world Schopenhauer came to see as purely and totally the objectification of a blind and impulsive Will in forms of ascending complexity, from primal forces of nature, the most inert substances (rock, stone), through the complete hierarchy of plant and animal life, to man himself – in whom the Will miraculously attains to consciousness of itself: consciousness of a world in which the outlook for the individual members of any one life-form (for Schopenhauer the Platonic 'Idea') is grim indeed. Nature, we are told, cares only for the species, the 'Idea', not the individuals. These individuals, as in a sense illusory entities split from the one and essentially indivisible Will, must inevitably be involved in continual conflict with one another. We are all heirs to the inevitable suffering which our very 'willing' must bring upon us in this respect, as we live out the lives of puppets, predestined by the inner clockwork spring of the Will, which drives us on to our necessary end as individuals. Only (and here Schopenhauer seminally appropriated the early nineteenth century's rediscovery of Eastern philosophy and religion to what he regarded as the 'true nature' of Christianity) by *denying* the Will, denying the illusory veil of 'Maya', might man (and man alone) seek "salvation": in the Prajna-Paramita of the Buddhists, which Schopenhauer unequivocally saw as an ultimate 'nothingness'. Here is Schopenhauer himself towards the end of Volume II of *The World as Will and Representation:*

> This world is the battle-ground of tormented and agonized beings who continue to exist only by each devouring the other. Therefore, every beast of prey in it is the living grave of thousands of others, and its self-maintenance is a chain of torturing deaths. Then in this world the capacity to feel pain increases with knowledge, and therefore reaches its highest degree in man, a degree that is the higher, the more intelligent the man. To this world the attempt has been made to adapt the system of *optimism*, and to demonstrate to us that it is the best of all possible worlds. The absurdity is glaring. However, an optimist tells me to open my eyes and look at the world and see how beautiful it is in the sunshine, with its mountains, valleys, rivers, plants, animals, and so on. But is the world, then, a peep-show? These things are certainly beautiful to *behold* but to *be* them is something quite different.[7]

* * *

I quote the above passage in full in order to try and illustrate in as lively a fashion as possible why Mahler – one of whose favourite novelists was Dostoyevsky and to whom, as the youthful wayfarer, the bird had once *fruitlessly* chirruped "see, is the world not lovely?"[8] – must indeed have wrestled with Schopenhauer's so frighteningly persuasive view of the world.

This Mahler was also, however, the composer of the Finale of the Second Symphony, the bells-and-angels movement of the Third – the Mahler who was to strive for the "positive and productive mood"[9] in the face of an entire generation of decadent 'negators' who, like Wagner, were apparently prepared to consign themselves to oblivion with the explicitly Schopenhauerian "black flag" that was to have flown at the end of *Tristan*.[10]

At the time of his engagement and marriage to Alma Schindler (1901–2), the now Roman Catholic Mahler (since 1897) seems to have relegated at least parts of Schopenhauer, along with Nietzsche, to the paraphernalia of the frivolous and superficial *fin de siècle* milieu from which he so urgently wished to liberate his young fiancée. In the extraordinary cards-on-the-table letter that Mahler wrote to her in December 1901, he dealt none too delicately with the intellectual pretensions she would appear to have laid before him:

> My little Alma, we must agree in *our love* and in our hearts! But in our ideas? My Alma! What are your ideas? Schopenhauer's chapter on women, the whole deceitful and viciously shameless immorality of Nietzsche's superiority of an élite, the turbid meanderings of Mæterlinck's drunken mind.... These, *thank God,* are not your ideas but theirs![11]

Alma herself was to indicate that her modern, 'free-thinking' adherence to both Nietzsche *and* Schopenhauer was strongly opposed by Mahler.[12]

Yet we should note that he fixes, in the above letter, upon one specific weak link in Schopenhauer (a point which Alma could not contest without bringing the whole matter rather disadvantageously down upon her own head!). The really strong guns are brought to bear upon Nietzsche.[13] Indeed, running contrary to the notion of Mahler's ever having become rootedly 'anti-Schopenhauer' is the knowledge, also derived from his wife's memoir, that he was fond of quoting one of Schopenhauer's quips about the effect of noise makers on the sensitive genius;[14] and there remains, of course, the high praise, indeed reverence, with which Mahler seems to have spoken about Schopenhauer's discussion of music.

★   ★   ★

Schopenhauer himself was to speak of the "bright and fair"[15] contents of Book III of the first volume of his major work (containing his philosophy of art), as compared with the general, pessimistic gloom of the rest. The reason for this becomes clear as we piece together his comments on the activity of, for example, the visual or plastic artist, whom he saw as attempting to get beyond the individualized object-manifestations of the Will (including his own) to the essential form, or 'Idea' of his subject. Schopenhauer regarded the artist as one who was miraculously able to sink himself into the world – to free himself from the time-obsessed involvement with his own Will, in pure (Will-freed) contemplation:

7

What kind of knowledge is it that considers what continues to exist outside and independently of all relations, but which alone is really essential to the world, the true content of its phenomena, that which is subject to no change, and is therefore known with equal truth for all time, in a word the *Ideas* that are the immediate and adequate objectivity of the thing-in-itself, of the will? It is *art*, the work of genius. It represents the eternal Ideas apprehended through pure contemplation, the essential and abiding element in all the phenomena of the world. According to the material in which it repeats, it is sculpture, painting, poetry or music. Its only source is knowledge of the Ideas; its sole aim is communication of this knowledge.[16]

While Schopenhauer's understanding of visual art is limited, we may see how it accommodates elements of Eastern thought in preparing the ground for his theoretical picture of the most highly estimable, and specifically *artistic* abilities of the 'genius':

For genius to appear in an individual, it is as if a measure of the power of knowledge must have fallen to his lot far exceeding that required for the service of an individual will; and this superfluity of knowledge having become free, now becomes the subject purified of will, the clear mirror of the inner nature of the world. This explains the animation, amounting to disquietude, in men of genius, since the present can seldom satisfy them, because it does not fill their consciousness.[17]

Nevertheless, they are miraculously able to attain (and communicate to us in the work of art, if we are truly receptive) to the essential stillness of "pure contemplation", which is generally denied to most mortals in the ceaseless cycle of their willing: "No attained object of willing can give a satisfaction that lasts and no longer declines; . . . without peace and calm true well-being is absolutely impossible. Thus the subject of willing is constantly lying on the revolving wheel of Ixion. . . ."[18]

Reminded here of the self-destructive compulsion of the Will itself, in the context of Schopenhauer's belief in the artist's power to transcend it (by literally transcending *himself* in time; the illusion of individuation), we are prepared somewhat for the novelty of his broadly metaphorical description of music, which, he tells us, "is by no means like the other arts, namely a copy of the Ideas, but a *copy of the will itself*": "For this reason the effect of music is so very much more powerful and penetrating than is that of the other arts, for these others speak only of the shadow, but music of the essence."[19]

In order to comprehend more fully what Schopenhauer means here, in according to music so high and special a place amongst the arts, we must recall how important the *self-consciousness* of man was to him: as the final coming to consciousness of the Will itself. By looking into himself, man could perceive the 'in-itself' of the world – the essentially one and indivisible Will of which his own separate individuation is but illusory, at best transitory. Schopenhauer built up his picture of the natural order of the world not by sifting the data of his senses, but by looking *within* himself. The individual's consciousness may (if he possesses some quality of genius as Schopenhauer understood it) thus become "a *camera obscura* in which the

9

macrocosm exhibits itself". But whereas 'perceiving' has space as its form,

> Our self-consciousness has ... only time; therefore our thinking does not, like our perceiving, take place in *three* dimensions, but merely in *one*, that is in a line, without breadth and depth. From this fact springs the greatest of our intellect's essential imperfections. We can know everything only *successively*. . . .[20]

We may now easily see how music, the only art-form which itself has time as its sole element, should have presented itself to Schopenhauer as the most direct and immediate expression of man's self-consciousness, or, as we might say, the Will's consciousness of itself. In the earlier sections of Volume II, in which Schopenhauer anticipates Freud with prodigious insight, we learn that

> consciousness is like a magic lantern, in the focus of which only one picture can appear at a time; and every picture, even when it depicts the noblest thing, must nevertheless soon vanish to make way for the most different and even the most vulgar thing.[21]

And here, a little earlier:

> Consciousness is the mere surface of our mind, and of this, as of the globe, we do not know the interior, but only the crust.
> But ... what puts into activity the association of ideas itself ... is the *will*. This drives its servant, the intellect, according to its powers to link one idea onto another, to recall the similar and the simultaneous, and to recognise grounds and consequents.[22]

It is in the light of such ideas as these that we might best see the logic behind Schopenhauer's description of, for example, a Beethoven symphony as "a true picture of the nature of the world, which rolls on in the boundless confusion of innumerable forms and maintains itself by constant destruction"[23] – or his otherwise apparently somewhat curious metaphorical elucidation of the inner significance of harmonic music based on the developed system of Western tonality. The deepest tones, the ground-bass, he sees as the articulation of "the lowest grades of the will's objectification, inorganic nature, the mass of the planet",[24] while as we move up through the inner voices (space precludes my dealing here with Schopenhauer's detailed ideas on rhythm and tempo, or harmony) we pass through the metaphorically articulated voices of the vegetable and animal kingdoms.

Finally, in the *melody*, in the high, singing, principal voice, leading the whole and progressing with unrestrained freedom, in the uninterrupted significant connexion of *one* thought from beginning to end, and expressing a whole, I recognize the highest grade of the will's objectification, the intellectual life and endeavour of man. He alone, because endowed with the faculty of reason, is always looking before and after on the path of his actual life and of its innumerable possibilities, and so achieves a course of life that is intellectual, and is thus connected as a whole. In keeping with this *melody* alone has significant and intentional connexion from beginning to end. Consequently, it relates the story of the intellectually enlightened will, the copy or impression whereof in actual life is the series of its deeds. Melody, however, says more; it relates the most secret history of the intellectually enlightened will, portrays every agitation, every effort, every movement of the will, everything which the faculty of reason summarizes under the wide and negative concept of feeling, and which cannot be further taken up into the abstraction of reason. Hence it has always been said that music is the language of feeling and passion, just as words are the language of reason.[25]

* * *

Well, we would not perhaps choose to write in quite this way today, but the general tenor of Schopenhauer's thought, against which I have set this remarkable passage, should help us to see more clearly how Mahler might have read it; finding in it a profound revelation of all that he was, all that he aspired to as a specifically Musician heir to the central European philosophical and artistic traditions. In *The World as Will and Representation*, Schopenhauer forged the ring through which both were to pass to come out metaphorically, if not actually, fused into one on the other side. At one point, for example, he compares scientific 'specialists' to

the musicians in an orchestra, each of whom is master of his own instrument; and the philosopher to the conductor, who must be acquainted with the nature and method of handling every instrument, yet without playing them all, or even only one of them, with great perfection.[26]

Knowing of his high estimation of it, we might legitimately use Schopenhauer's discussion of the nature of music as a portal through which to pass to a fuller understanding of Mahler's belief in the profound significance of his own art. In this way we might attain to a deeper comprehension, perhaps, of his special position at the end of the nineteenth century as the archetypal philosopher-conductor, who was also the composer of the Third Symphony, of colossal symphonic streams of consciousness like the Fifth's second movement or its Scherzo (of which Mahler wrote to Alma: "Oh, heavens, what are they to make of this chaos of which new worlds are for ever being engendered, only to crumble in ruins the moment after? . . ."[27]), or of the Finale of the Sixth – in which most Schopenhauerian of all Mahler's symphonic movements, the fruitlessly and yet frantically heavenwards-aspiring individuation of the will is thrice crushed by mighty axe-strokes. We might say that in Mahler's music, as already in Wagner's to some considerable extent, Schopenhauer's metaphor becomes reality in a way that could well have surprised the philosopher, although his comprehension of Beethoven should have made the transition possible. For Mahler was no gentleman of the Enlightenment, prepared to sing the song of Reason to the accompaniment of the ground-bass of gravity and the ticking counterpoint of a well-ordered clockwork universe (as, even in spite of himself, Schopenhauer's metaphor might at times be read). In his works, Mahler not only illustrated, but emotionally and intellectually *confronted* Schopenhauer's world-picture, being as a musician as able and prepared as the philosopher to plunge beneath the surface of human consciousness; to attempt to articulate, at all stages of its objectification, the voice of the Will: to create, quite literally, a world in music, in which man was in no way denied his supreme, if agonizing, role as the 'perceiving', singing consciousness in the midst of it all – whose connected song of awareness is unfolded most fully in the great Adagios of which Mahler (precisely employing one of Schopenhauer's own images, quoted above) was to say to Natalie Bauer-Lechner:

> "In the Adagio, everything is resolved into quiet 'being'; the Ixion-wheel of appearances has at last been brought to a standstill. . . . So, contrary to custom – and without knowing why at the time – I concluded my Second and Third Symphonies with Adagios: that is, with a higher as opposed to a lower form."[28]

★   ★   ★

In the first volume of *The World as Will and Representation*, Schopenhauer makes the following claim: ". . . a perfectly accurate and complete explanation of music which goes into detail, and thus a detailed repetition in concepts of what it expresses, this would also be at once a sufficient repetition and explanation of the world in concepts."[29] Now if we chose to analyse the Finale of Mahler's Sixth in this way, it would indeed be a depressingly Schopenhauerian world that was elucidated – evidence as important in its way as any of the statements cited earlier as indications of the nature and extent of Mahler's philosophical affinity with Schopenhauer. Yet the Mahler of the Finale of the Seventh Symphony, of the Eighth, would surely have been profoundly disturbed at any such conclusion. We should, of course, rather say that it is the composer's specific view of the world at the time of writing his music that may be represented in it. Had Schopenhauer known more than he did about the music of his own day, and about the wider history of music, he would surely have recognized this flaw in his theory. If, indeed, we attempt to read it with the eyes of a European at the end of the nineteenth century, we might well find ourselves inclined to overlook the ropes by which it is moored to the mainland of Schopenhauer's own view of the world, and admire primarily the comprehension it otherwise so clearly embodies: of an art-form which is potentially the most intimate and direct representation of the individual consciousness, on the level of its most essential reality, and in the very element of that consciousness, namely Time. This certainly lies at the heart of what Schopenhauer has to tell us about music: "For only the passions, the movements of the will, exist for it, and, like God, it sees only the heart."[30] – and this Will was already in part becoming conceptually meta-morphosed into the Freudian unconscious, the 'id', in a way that would once again sunder man from nature; from the in-itself of the larger world. In his Eighth Symphony, Mahler was in fact possibly the last to celebrate a conceptual unity of inner and outer nature, to the extent that the Will takes on there the aspect of the impulsive, even explicitly sexual *Eros*, which nevertheless includes *Caritas*[31] (the *Liebe* of the Third) and is a positive spirit of boundless creation as much as a force for inevitable destruction.

While a comparison between the final "ewig, ewig!" paean of the Eighth's *Chorus mysticus*, and the dying, fading reiteration of the same word at the end of the work which immediately followed it, reminds us that Mahler's struggle against Schopenhauerian pessimism was never quite conclusively won, it is also worth pointing out that, for all its heterophonic *chinoiserie*, *Das Lied von der Erde* offers no world-rejecting dissolution of the veils of Maya. Not even a nihilistic, Schopenhauerian redemption is permitted in this intellectually chastened expressive act that embodies the now almost exclusively subjective vision of Mahler's last existential crisis. Yet for all that the invocation of a consoling *Deus ex machina* is eschewed here, this is still no music that denies its own all too human nature in becoming the guilty hostage of an idea. The death of the individual that is symbolized in this conclusion no more entails the death of music than it entails a denial of the however unbearably alluring reality of the world that is being left. For the "song of sorrow" has been sung out to the last, barely audible D of the archetypal expressive sighs whose resolution on the tonic C is left to the accompanying instruments. They sustain it not in a conventional C major triad, however, but a crystalline added-sixth chord (coloured by flute, harp and celesta – a combination of instruments reserved by Mahler for children and angels). It still bears Mahler's wonder at just such a spring dawn as that in which he had first awakened as a symphonic composer long ago "in the days of youth". The tragically painful realism of this duality holds the key not only to this work, but also to the special achievement of Mahler's two succeeding symphonies. For the extremity and vulnerability of their expressive anguish must retrospectively be seen to contain an example and challenge more vital and more positive by far than he himself may have suspected when he looked at the manuscript of *Das Lied von der Erde* with Bruno Walter and asked him: "What do you think? Is this to be endured at all? Will not people make away with themselves after hearing it?"[32]

TWO

Strauss's Transfiguration

Strauss, in no sense a supporter of the Jews,
always stressed (even during Mahler's lifetime)
that certain ones, like Mahler, meant a great deal
to him. He was, however, always "a little fright-
ened by him". We naturally went on to lament
his early death. Strauss then observed that
Mahler had always sought redemption. He had
simply no idea what kind of redemption Mahler
was thinking of. Strauss's precise words were: "I
do not understand what I am supposed to be
redeemed from. If I can sit down at my desk in
the morning and get some sort of inspiration,
then I certainly do not need redemption as well.
What did Mahler mean by it?"[1]

On the face of it, this little anecdote of Otto Klemperer's, relating to the summer of 1911, strikingly
reinforces what one might call the official late
twentieth-century attitude towards Strauss. His music
is as popular as that of any of his European
contemporaries, and has become the subject of
increasing scholarly attention. Yet even his strongest
adherents admit that, as both man and artist, he had a
number of flaws which cannot, alas, be overlooked. In
terms of the idealized image of the Artist still

preferred within the cultural context in which he worked, he was much too much of a pragmatist. At certain periods of his life he appeared even frankly to prostitute his art in a way that suggests at best a certain shallowness of temperament, at worst, vulgarity – and this even granted that we overlook the unfortunate business of his dealings with the Nazis.

Moral judgements about artists, however, have a curious way of reflecting more upon the judge than the judged, and even on the level of the purely aesthetic criticisms that have been levelled at Strauss, there are involved a number of assumptions that we would do well to examine periodically – just to make sure that we mean what we think we are saying. What is worrying about the 'official' Strauss criticism in which we have all invested to a greater or lesser degree, is not simply the way in which it may function as an excuse for responsible thought, but more specifically the way in which it is manoeuvred to support the view that Strauss was a reactionary composer, a conservative. In the sense that he went on writing tonal music to the end of his life (and almost to the end of Schoenberg's, therefore!) the label is not to be disputed. Yet if we consider him conservative to the extent that he evaded the issues of his time we are doing him an injustice. It is the nature of this injustice that I propose to address here.

★ ★ ★

Klemperer's anecdote is useful for the way in which it strikes to the heart of Strauss's creative personality, of his very attitude towards art. This attitude may be discerned precisely in his mystification about 'redemption'. Was he merely being maliciously whimsical? There is no question that Mahler represents at least a *kind* of artist that Klemperer might have expected Strauss to venerate. Really to be mystified by the notion of *Erlösung* (Redemption) would be to lack a very basic tool for dealing with the whole nineteenth-century Germanic tradition, stretching back to Beethoven and Goethe. Whether we like it or not, there was an awful lot of 'redemption' floating about in the world of Strauss's creative forebears. Wagner, a composer Strauss never, to my knowledge, claimed not to understand, was more or less obsessed by it in various forms, and had ended his creative career blissfully envisaging 'Erlösung dem Erlöser!' (Redemption to the Redeemer!). The metaphysical *Angst* which forms the very core of Mahler's particular kind of post-Wagnerian art can hardly be brushed aside as merely an idiosyncratic appendage to his creative work. The particular answers that Mahler was to synthesize in the face of the great questions of life that he posed in the first movement of the Second Symphony are central to any assessment of his stature, precisely because they reflect upon a central tension in European thought that was straining to crisis point on many different levels at this time. It is surely no accident that Strauss himself, ever sensitive to the prevailing wind, should have produced a tone-poem entitled *Death and Transfiguration* precisely during that period when Mahler was wondering how, if ever, he might continue his Second Symphony – which existed in 1890 only in the form of a single initial movement entitled *Todtenfeier* (Funeral Rites). What, then, was Strauss getting at by dissociating himself from the need for redemption?

My suggestion is that we should read Klemperer's anecdote not as evidence of Strauss's Bavarian boorishness, but rather of a conscious standpoint that he had adopted by 1911, concerning the nature of art and German music and influenced no doubt by Nietzsche as much as Hofmannsthal. It is a standpoint that Mahler himself would have understood – although this is not to deny that there existed a radical temperamental difference between the two composers (Mahler himself once put it that he and Strauss were tunnelling into the same mountain from diametrically opposite directions[2]). It is the difference between the prophetic martyr and the born survivor. Something of my point can be made precisely by comparing and contrasting the different kinds of 'redemption' envisaged by Mahler and Strauss respectively in the Second Symphony and *Tod und Verklärung*.

In a way the relative dimensions of the two works are crucial – and the length of Mahler's symphony also entails a remarkable element of real time: the period of years that elapsed between the composition of the *Todtenfeier* (1888) and the completion of the great Finale in 1894. We know that this period – certainly its latter part – represented a time of inner questioning for Mahler, who had put the mighty questions of the first movement ("What is life – and what is death?"[3]) in the form of an evolving dialectical conflict between outbursts of god-defying energy and dreamlike visions

of fragile beauty that are linked only by the sepulchral
tread of a funeral procession. The First Symphony
bears witness to the fact that Mahler cannot have been
at a loss for musical means whereby to transform or
'transfigure' this fatal march into the winging
resurrection-song of the concluding chorus. The fact
that he needed also an *intellectual* justification
(connected with the problem of the programme and
the matter of a suitable text to set) for wielding the
magical affective power of music in this way, defines
precisely what was most tensely modern about
Mahler's art and what led him to observe that it was
'lived' to an extent that could not be appreciated by
those who had not for themselves experienced "the
raging gales of our great epoch".[4]

In contrast, we might put it that Strauss proves
himself able, already in *Tod und Verklärung*, to
content himself with the magic and leave the philosophy, the 'living' in Mahler's sense, to others.
Whereas the sheer irreconcilability of the two worlds
in the first movement of Mahler's Second gives to its
concluding collapse a gloomy authenticity that renders
the Finale all the more remarkable, Strauss's tone-
poem is unquestionably bottom heavy. We sense that
the whole thing grew out of the lovely rising arc of the
'idealism' theme (or however we label it) which it is
the business of the piece as a whole to enshrine in a
musico-dramatic context that shows it off to its best
advantage. It and the lyrical motives of the 'friendly
dreams' of his childhood are what live in our memory,
rather than the stagey clamour of the Allegro's 'striv-
ing and passions', whose character and musical role as

sonata first-subject group seem all too clearly modelled upon Tchaikovsky's *Romeo and Juliet* fantasy-over-ture. Indeed, contrary to Norman del Mar's insistence on the importance of a preconceived, elaborately detailed programmatic scenario,[5] I would suggest that *Tod und Verklärung* is interesting and successful primarily as a formal experiment in transformation in a post-Beethovenian, extended-coda sonata form of precisely the kind that Mahler had used in the Finale of his First Symphony – and even here, programme or no, Strauss is unable to prevent a standard recapitulation from starting to get under way at bar 378.

One might put it that Mahler's enigmatically expressed and latterly concealed programmes are far more important to a full comprehension of the nature and structure of his symphonies than Strauss's gleefully publicized scenarios to an appreciation of his symphonic poems – and precisely for the reason that Mahler's works are 'lived' in the way indicated above. Relying upon the extraordinary alchemical experimentation and researches of Wagner, both composers were musical magicians of a very high order. Yet if the relationship between Mahler and Strauss is rather like that of the Sorcerer and the Apprentice in the famous tale, we would in all fairness have to observe that while he may never quite have comprehended the Sorcerer's reverence for his arts, based on a profound respect (born of arcane experience) for the forces he invoked, Strauss certainly knew how to control his broomsticks. And in that knowledge he was ready and able to offer himself as a magician for hire.

We are returned to the question of sincerity, although I would now wish to approach it on a rather more serious level than the more familiar one that concerns itself with Strauss's having conducted in 'Wanamaker's' and ended his life selling bits of his manuscripts to American tourists. For we are almost in a position to observe that Strauss, apparently immune to the dangers of the magic powers of late nineteenth-century music, was able to wield them with precisely that kind of directness and naiveté that other nineteenth-century composers, Mahler not least among them, came to associate with an image of Mozart – the composer who had provided early romantic writers like E. T. A. Hoffmann with a paradigm of the divine genius who could 'let go', who could escape from the chaos of reality into the wittily and passionately articulated order of the ideal realm of Music. The late nineteenth century's resuscitation of this image had not a little to do with the feelings that had prompted Nietzsche to advocate the 'mediterraneanization' of art, specifically music, in the dense wake of Wagner. Few European artists who had been established at the turn of the century and who lived beyond the First World War did so with the feeling that everything could go on as it had before. By following something of a Nietzschean path, rather than the more darkly Faustian one of Schoenberg, Strauss demonstrated a highly idiosyncratic version of the however necessary metamorphosis of the nineteenth-century artist into the twentieth-century composer. What path of change Mahler might have followed can only be conjectured. The fact remains that Strauss survived two World Wars and planted the *Four*

Last Songs in the very middle of the twentieth century; and I do not speak of merely physical survival here.

★   ★   ★

Richard Strauss concert at Lamoureux's. – A young man, tall and thin, curly hair with a tonsure which begins at the crown of the head, a fair moustache, pale eyes and face. Less the head of a musician than that of any provincial squireen. . . . He conducted Beethoven's Symphony in A major, the Prelude to *Lohengrin* and the overture to *Die Meistersinger*, and his symphonic poem *Also sprach Zarathustra*. He conducts waywardly, abruptly, dramatically, in the same style as Wagner. . . . Taken all in all, more a strong man than an inspired one. Vital force, nerves, a morbid over-excitement, a lack of balance which will-power holds in check, but which disturbs the music and the musician. It was enough to see him at the end of the Beethoven symphony, his great body twisted askew as if struck by both hemiplegia and St. Vitus's dance at the same time, his fists clenched and contorted, knock-kneed, tapping with his foot on the dais – to feel the malady hidden beneath the power and the military stiffness . . .

Well, well! I've got an idea that Germany will not keep the equilibrium of omnipotence for long – In her brain there are dizzy promptings. Nietzsche, R. Strauss, the Kaiser Wilhelm . . . there's Neroism in the air.[6]

Here, through the eyes of Romain Rolland, we see the *fin de siècle* Strauss very much in the thick of things. Indeed, Rolland has him whirling at the very centre of the maelstrom of German 'Neroism' that showed every sign of sucking the highest principles of Western art, perhaps even the whole of Western culture, into its vortex. Rolland and others had scented the same sacrilegious madness in Mahler. Artistic subject-matter had bounded from the constraints of bourgeois taste and the means of expression were riotiously multiplying to the point where nothing was apparently forbidden. Strauss himself would shortly set Salome on stage to oppose John the Baptist's renunciant and Wagnerian absorption in the 'mystery of death' with the Nietzschean 'mystery of life', whose song she would nevertheless sing as a daemonic, Secessionist Isolde, slithering in gore made audible in the unbridled chromaticism of a musical language whose veils had been shed long before Salome's in her famous dance.

Here was a language less of the Schopenhauerian Will than the Freudian unconscious. From the first inception of Goethe's *Faust* to Mahler's setting of its final scene in the Eighth Symphony, the German tradition had been dominated by the hero 'animus' in search of an ideal heroine 'anima'. Now, however, the eternally faithful Gretchen has turned man-eater (and how closely is Salome related to Puccini's Turandot!). Eros itself has become a suicidal force of disillusionment. And nowhere is the death-wish more starkly manifest than in Strauss's next heroine: the hell-bent Elektra. Her frenzied dance of suicidal death-lust not fortuitously recalls the ride of the Valkyrie maidens as they retrieve the souls of dead warriors. We might see Strauss's Elektra as a latterday Brünnhilde who, traumatized by the death of her father-god Wotan (Sophocles' Agamemnon), is now concerned only to do to death all subsequent impostors, her murderous mother and even herself. Life has become for her no more than the desire for cataclysmic revenge upon a world that would not allow her to remain a child.

The final great duologue (it is emphatically *not* a dialogue) of Elektra and her sister Chrysothemis sets terminal ecstasy against the joy of new hope. There can be no tomorrow for Elektra, who has focused her entire life upon her desire for this act of revenge that could be accomplished only by her long-exiled brother Orestes. Now it is done, and the fire of her exultation must consume her. Chrysothemis, on the contrary, has continually longed for escape from the prison of her mother's house and her sister's passion. She may appear weak by comparison with Elektra, and yet she it is who bears within her the seeds of the future: longing for a life in which she might fulfil herself as a woman and a mother; might help to turn the wheel of destiny that for Elektra has ceased for ever. "Life is beginning for you and me and for all men," cries Chrysothemis against Elektra's ". . . the fire of life and my flame is burning up the darkness of. the world". The opera may be Elektra's, but it is Chryso-themis who realizes that the world depends upon contrast and contrariety; that without darkness there can be no light; that Elektra's hysterical illumination can but prelude a total eclipse.

★ ★ ★

The Strauss of these early years of the twentieth
century is logically enough the Strauss who en-
couraged the young Arnold Schoenberg and even suggested *Pelléas et Mélisande* as a possibly fruitful subject for him. Schoenberg would shortly produce the
monodrama *Erwartung*, in which the demented shade
of Salome and Elektra wanders off alone into the dark
forest of the unconscious, 'searching' – perhaps for her
Tristan, her John the Baptist, whose corpse she had
stumbled upon but which she leaves behind at the last
without remorse. The forest into which she wandered
was also that of the ascetic and relentless modernism
into which Schoenberg himself was to venture on a
steeply rising path that rapidly left Strauss behind on
the foothills, barely even on the forest's edge. For
what did Strauss turn to after *Elektra*? *Der
Rosenkavalier*, *Ariadne auf Naxos*, the *Alpine
Symphony* – oh dear no; this way the twentieth century
did not lie! Or did it?

It is at this juncture in his career that Strauss is
reckoned to have fallen away from the high modernist
path. Indeed he did; but it is precisely here that the
criteria of 'progress' must be examined most carefully.
I have already posed the question whether in fact
Strauss can be regarded as an artist who evaded the
issues of his time. We have seen that the Strauss of
Tod und Verklärung, of *Salome* and *Elektra* was certainly not doing that, whatever our final aesthetic
judgement about the quality of some of his music may
be. What is so curious about the 'official' reading of
his subsequent career is that it relies totally upon the
history of musico-linguistic innovation for its notions

of where the most consequential line of progress lay.

An enormous problem looms here, whose articulation and solution lie outside the scope of the present essay. It is nevertheless possible to suggest that our criteria of 'progress' might equally well rely upon what it is that survives the necessary processes of historical change as upon a quantitative analysis of the mechanics of such change. Perhaps what I am trying to suggest here is that if we opt for Chrysothemis as our heroine rather than Elektra, then we might well see Schoenberg as the more limited, 'period' phenomenon, and specifically in terms of the model of the German Artist to which he subscribed. The Strauss of *Der Rosenkavalier* and *Ariadne auf Naxos* could well be considered to have realized Chrysothemis' dream and *escaped* from the claustrophobic and obsessive atmosphere of his forebears' house. Conservative as his musical language may have been, it is really a startlingly transfigured Strauss who, having composed the new Prologue to *Ariadne*, could write to Hofmannsthal in 1913 as follows:

> Your cry of pain against Wagnerian music manufacture has gone deep into my heart and has pushed open the door to a quite new landscape in which, led by *Ariadne*, especially the new Prologue, I hope to make my way along the path of an entirely un-Wagnerian opera of action, mood and humanity. I now see the way clearly before me, and thank you for opening my eyes. . . . I promise you that I have now cast off the whole musical armour of Wagner for ever.[7]

★　★　★

I have described Strauss as a 'born survivor', somewhat in the context of a rehearsal of the familiar
accusations of vulgar pragmatism and a certain
shallowness. Perhaps it was these very qualities that
saved him. Romain Rolland, whose 1898 diagnosis
of 'Neroism' I have quoted, was subsequently led
to suggest that Strauss was if anything *less* the nervously unstable decadent than Mahler, observing that
Strauss "knows how to relax. Excitable and at the
same time somnolent, he escapes from his state of
nerves by his power of inertia; there is an underlying
Bavarian indolence in him."[8] Of course, looked at
another way, we might wish to see this 'power of
inertia' linked to a certain lack of commitment to
the role of Artist (*did* Strauss perhaps care more
for his skat games?) that inspired in Mahler a devotion somewhat akin to that of both the priest and
the research physicist to their own respective pursuits. How else could Strauss have brought himself
to degrade the magical arts that Mahler had employed for probing the ultimate mysteries of life to
the extent of using them to bath the baby and sort
out a family quarrel in the *Sinfonia Domestica* of
1903?

The point is that Strauss's survival is of interest,
indeed importance, precisely for the reason that he
survived with so much. To regard *Der Rosenkavalier*
as the indulgence of a faint-hearted, perhaps com-
mercially-minded conservative is both culturally naive
and critically small-minded. For here at last was something of that 'mediterraneanization' of Germanic,
Wagnerian art that Nietzsche had once advocated. But

instead of a leap in the direction of Stravinskian neo-
classicism or Schoenberg's alternative brand of wilful
linguistic self-limitation, Strauss managed to achieve
his own rebirth as a composer closer to the nineteenth
century's long-courted image of the 'divine Mozart'
than either Tchaikovsky or Mahler – to take two great
nineteenth-century Mozartians – had ever been permitted to realize in their own works.

There is in *Der Rosenkavalier* "action, mood and
humanity" in plenty – I would even be inclined to
suggest that it is the first work in which Strauss's
precocious genius found its real level – and it was
paradoxically only after his final conscious rejection of
the image of the Wagnerian redemption-seeker that he
began to mature as an Artist in the highest sense (the
slow maturing of a prodigy who is destined to live long
enough to realize his early promise). The creator of
the final scene of *Der Rosenkavalier* was an artist more
universal in his humanity, less linked to the moods
and crises and stylistic peculiarities of a particular
period than almost any other Western composer of the
twentieth century; and if that is his triumph, it has
also been his undoing. The 'modern man' of any age
perhaps likes to feel that his own predicament and
vision are unique in their complexity and totality, and
demand a unique language in which to be expressed.
That Strauss should have gone on to say new things
about perennial problems and predicaments in the
vernacular was an affront to the self-proclaimed
progressives who sided with the hell-bent Elektra
without a thought for the fact that a canny Chryso-

themis might yet salvage a life from the wreckage of her youthful dreams.

*   *   *

Perhaps the deeper worry that has shadowed critical disapproval of Strauss registers the fact that his physical survival from the 'old world' was matched by social survival in the new as a composer with an audience; as a composer who had effectively salvaged nineteenth-century bourgeois music for a new bourgeoisie of the twentiety century. Rather than rejecting the particular social and cultural circumstances in which he found himself and aspiring for some transcendent creative authenticity, Strauss appeared to revel in those circumstances. Following the shade of Chrysothemis out of expressionistic opera and into the middle-class domesticity of *Arabella* and *Intermezzo*, he replaced the mythical or symbolic heroine with a real woman, even with his own wife, in the midst of whose jealous rages and petty whims a spark of elemental passion may yet be discerned. Such passion would find its highest expression in those stratospherically winging songs of ecstatic rationality with which Strauss blessed all his later heroines, from the Marschallin onwards, in works which represent a last logical step in the bourgeois appropriation of grand opera.

Compared with the knife-edged awareness and high artistic aims of Mahler, the early Strauss cut a modish but somewhat diminutive figure. Yet if on one level he appeared the travelling salesman in post-Wagnerian musical effects, there was something of quality in the scurrilous lightness with which he publicly wore the mantle of 'hero' in his works. There is certainly an inner consistency in the way in which this hero, while always revealing Strauss's own gait and inimitable manner, exchanged the masks of Don Juan and Till Eulenspiegel for that of Nietzsche's Zarathustra, and then dropped even that one in *Ein Heldenleben* and the *Sinfonia Domestica*. Chameleon he may have appeared, but Strauss was all along in reality a slowly evolving caterpillar, whose own 'transfiguration' at around the time of Mahler's death was to see him emerge at last as a new kind of artist.

It might be suggested that in such pressing circumstances as we must now go on to analyse more closely, Strauss's creative transformation represented precisely a kind of 'redemption'. One might put it paradoxically as the suggestion that only by rejecting the Mahlerian earnestness (as it was, perhaps, in his indolent, Bavarian nature to do) did Strauss manage to survive the comprehensive catastrophes of the first decades of the twentieth century and emerge as an artist whose range of utterance, of sheer humanity, in a New World could match that of Mahler's in the Old. Certainly the weakness of the standard critical attitude towards this consummately realized art of unashamedly bourgeois, democratic liberalism, has been that it has failed to face up to the social and even political premises upon which its argument rests. Neither the purely linguistic nor the mysteriously 'aesthetic' arguments otherwise get very close to the heart of the matter.

THREE

The Problem of *Doctor Faustus*

> *The artist is the brother of the criminal and the madman. Do you ween that any important work was ever wrought except its maker learned to understand the way of the criminal and the madman? Morbid and healthy! Without the morbid would life all its whole life never have survived. Genuine and false! Are we land-loping knaves? Do we draw the good things out of the nose of nothing? Where nothing is there the Devil too has lost his right and no pallid Venus produces anything worthwhile!*
>
> Thomas Mann: *Doctor Faustus*[1]

Thomas Mann's late novel (it was first published in 1947), for all its complexities and wilful, ironic subtleties, is grimly clear in what it has to say about the potential ambivalence of the role of artist in our time. What is remarkable is that he regarded this novel, whose hero is a signally ambivalent artist on a self-willed path to spiritual and even physical annihilation, as a "passionate and telling dramatization of our tragedy".[2] Furthermore, his artist, whose own personal

35

and creative tragedy is set against Nazi Germany's role as agent in the broader tragedy of modern European civilization, is specifically a composer. True, Mann explained that Leverkühn had been synthesized from a host of European artists and intellectuals of the nineteenth and early twentieth centuries, of whom only some were in fact musicians (the philosopher Nietzsche supplied the broad outline of Adrian Leverkühn's life). Yet Leverkühn's fictional works and attitudes are not merely diagnostic. So prophetic are they of the actual works and attitudes of subsequent European composers that one is taken aback by the implications. Either Mann's analysis and prognostications were simply the correct ones – in which case the mainstream of modern European music takes on the aspect of a laborious series of parerga to a novel – or we are faced by the unlikely prospect of real artists being influenced by a fictional one.

It would be as well to be more precise about the area of twentieth-century music that would appear to be both invoked and anticipated in Leverkühn's career. Apart from the considerable territory defined by the powerful influence of both Schoenberg and Stravinsky (with which two composers Adorno was primarily concerned in the *Philosophy of Modern Music*, read by Mann while he was working on the novel) other figures and tendencies might be referred to. Bartók's apparently highly developed concern for mathematical proportion and the timing and number of bars of often the smallest sections of musical movements comes to mind. Works by Penderecki, Lutozlawski, Ligeti and others contain many passages to which elements of the description of Leverkühn's apocalyptic oratorio could be applied. Quotation, parody and pastiche came to form the stock-in-trade of a generation of student composers in the wake of the fox-trots and medieval polyphony of Peter Maxwell Davies, or the background sources of Luciano Berio. The entire aleatory movement found its perhaps most coherent and philosophically articulate exponent in the 1950s with John Cage (a pupil of Schoenberg's in the city where *Doctor Faustus* was written), who could be said to have taken to its logical conclusion Adrian Leverkühn's sense of dissatisfaction at the lie of formal extension in 'the work'. Suggesting by implication that the initial inspiration or *Einfall* itself is in essence a lie of a similar sort, Cage renounced the fashionable refuge in mathematical organization along with the very concepts of form and content. His 'works' became in one sense a humble mystical invitation to Nature herself (as 'Chaos' in Cage's philosophy) to speak to us.

The paradox whereby an imaginary composer seems to command a central position in modern music is perhaps to be resolved less by recalling Mann's frequent references to the 'musical' aspects of his own literary technique, than by considering his admission that *Doctor Faustus* was, in large measure, an autobiographical work in which the daemonic composer and his humorously drawn, bourgeois biographer Serenus Zeitblom (in whose somewhat pedantic manner the story is narrated) were "secretly conceived as being identical with each other"[3] – or rather, perhaps, as two sides of his own personality. Yet to accept the close community of European arts in the early twentieth century, or even the notion of a *Zeitgeist* upon which Mann clearly relies, only heightens the problem that the novel presents us with if we accept the remarkable, broader consistency of the fiction and the reality. Whether Leverkühn takes his place alongside the real protagonists of our century specifically as a composer or as an artist in a vaguer and more general sense, the fact remains that he merits this place primarily by virtue of the disturbingly articulate logic with which Mann furnishes him. Aside from all the paraphernalia of irony, antithesis and post-Freudian psychological intimations that are the very stuff of Mann's literary style, aside even from the elaborate evocation of the Faust legend, whose long-established mythic potency for the West Mann is in a sense upending and attempting to terminate (Leverkühn is initially a Faust by fatal ordination rather than choice – he is a doomed Faust by birthright) – aside from all this, Leverkühn, through Zeitblom, articulates a precise awareness of how and why he becomes the artist he does; an awareness not wholly determined by the imaginative machinery of the novel. It is both compelling and shocking: compelling because it explains more satisfactorily and comprehensively than any real artist has been able to do the strangeness of much that is most strange in twentieth-century art; shocking because to accept this explanation is to accept that previous Western criteria regarding the value and nature of artistic achievement can no longer apply.

The problem of *Doctor Faustus* consists in the need to confront the purely intellectual premises of Leverkühn's artistic development and to consider whether the creative and philosophical conclusions he draws from them are indeed as logical and fatally inevitable as Mann would apparently have us believe. We must first, however, consider the nineteenth century's post-Darwinian notion of evolutionary progress and the way in which it was pressed into service by the first apologists of modernism, whose initial manifestations in music were as problematic as in any other art-form.

★　★　★

I must reject completely the five orchestral pieces of 1909. It is a tragicomic spectacle to see Schoenberg conducting this crazy cat music, urging on the players with an entranced or despairing expression on his face. These sounds conjure up hideous visions; monstrous apparitions threaten – there is nothing of joy and light, nothing that makes life worth living! How miserable would our descendents be, if this joyless, gloomy Schoenberg would ever become the mode of expression of their time! Is this destined to be the art of the future????

Hugo Leichtentritt, *Signale*, Berlin, 1912[4]

Innumerable writers, both critical and creative, have registered the apparent descent of an iron curtain of the spirit across the hitherto naturally developing 'progress' of the arts of the West in the first two decades of the twentieth century. As at the time, for example, of Schoenberg's first 'free atonal' works, or of his initial essays in 'composition with twelve tones', the least hostile members of their perplexed audiences turned first to the artists responsible, for elucidation and assistance. They were given to understand that the world of art in which they had hitherto felt at home – by virtue of being refreshed by it, entertained, erotically indulged, spiritually uplifted or whatever – was sustained by creative 'geniuses'. These mysterious beings, living atop the mountains of human feeling, spiritual awareness and philosophic speculation, were undergoing a process of natural development of their own. A logical and inevitable process was leading them away from the world of lower mortals that they had once chanced to indulge. The model invoked was apparently the old one of necessary change and innovation of the sort (as we recall) that had alienated audiences, patrons and public to varying degrees throughout the history of art. 'But such innovation as this?' (the bereft public asked of Schoenberg). In response the gods bestowed a revelation of divine wisdom. After all, it was not they who had wilfully effected the change, which was even a little painful to them (though, as gods, they gladly bore for mankind the burden of necessary suffering): instead, the artistic language had itself been dying. Internal decay had set in as a result of over-use and extravagant exploitation. In music, the very language that had sufficed, in its various stages of development, for the better part of a millenium, was bankrupt, played out, sterile.

Or so, at least, the revelation was communicated to

the populace and to music historians by acolytes and critic-mediums. Mann undoubtedly uses it as his starting-point in *Doctor Faustus*, if only to turn it on its head and suggest that it is artists, and not art, who are affected by decay. Yet beyond this extends his more profound and central analysis of the problem that could, in a special sense, be seen to oppose the irony in the above picture and demonstrate that the new artist, as we had secretly believed of the old, does indeed follow, on behalf of us all, a necessary path of suffering.

The secret lies in what he has to say about sterility and bankruptcy – not so much in the analysis by Adrian Leverkühn of the state of art, as his intellectual experience of what he feels he can honestly allow himself to do as artist. We soon begin to realize that for the tragic hero of the book (as Mann described him[5]) the problem is that of twentieth-century *awareness* – of 'what we now know' – before ever it is a problem of twentieth-century *art*. And indeed, the book flirts with the suggestion that the resolution of the problem of knowing and doing might well have led Leverkühn to seek redemption by abjuring the (fatally) culturally predetermined role of Artist altogether.

The intellectual basis of the problem is clearly revealed in Leverkühn's letter to Wendell Kretschmar in Chapter 15. Ever quick to grasp and see through things, he has come now to see through music, to see how it works and achieves its effects, to the extent that all that had once been perceived of these effects and attributed to 'inspiration' and 'genius' is drained of any mystical quality. He sees how it is all done and gets the hang of the "trick" of it: "Why does almost everything seem to me like its own parody? Why must I think that almost all, no, all the methods and conventions of art today *are good for parody only?*"[6] Thus Leverkühn, in the end half-heartedly, parries Kretschmar's efforts to draw him away from the (little less satisfactory to him) realms of theology and back into music. And it is indeed as that of a wilful, if superficially discreet, parodist that Leverkühn's own musical voice is most clearly heard in the novel for the first time. The work in question, the elaborately Debussyan symphonic fantasy *Ocean Lights*, astonishes Zeitblom as "a remarkable instance of how an artist can give his best to a thing in which he privately no longer believes, insisting on excelling in artistic devices which for his consciousness are already at the point of being worn out."[7] His subsequent assessment of Leverkühn's involvement with the work is crucial: "In truth parody was here the proud expedient of a great gift threatened with sterility by a combination of scepticism, intellectual reserve, and a sense of the deadly extension of the kingdom of the banal."[8]

Precisely in that the impossibility of attaining metaphysical knowledge was impressed upon Adrian Leverkühn by his Halle experiences, he is living out to the bitter end the great dilemma that was brought down upon the head of Western man by Kant in his demonstration that while faith and knowledge cannot be confused, it may be as advisable to indulge in the former as it is to pursue the latter within its proper bounds. Of all the conventional Faustian aspirations, that for Truth could be said to loom largest in Leverkühn's mind (artistic creativity he is in a sense pushed towards as a secondary, more immediate goal which in any event turns out to be the Devil's business). This truth he not surprisingly finds first within the pure, intellectually self-defined realm of mathematics. All else, particularly in the expressive arts, can be but *Schein* and ambivalence to a thinking contemporary of Freud and successor to Nietzsche; at least, such things *are not what we once thought them to be*.

The sense of disillusionment is of central importance. The Third Act prelude to *Die Meistersinger* might affect us as the comforting and moving revelation of a divine sort of wisdom and truth, expressed in a language necessarily removed from, or 'above' that of everyday life; but for Leverkühn, as man of his age par excellence, comprehension of the musical techniques (harmonic rhythm, melodic structure, the subtle dove-tailing of affective gestures) in fact *drains* the mystical quality from this supposedly most magical and mystical of art-forms. The mental and physiological effect turns out to be just that – *effect*, wilfully produced, whose content is in reality nothing more than the means to producing that effect. How can we delude ourselves into thinking any longer that the composer simply 'speaks out' what is within him in his chosen language? The famous Wordsworthian phrase, which is really about the Apolline working of Dionysian material, must now apparently be changed to "emotion *fabricated* in tranquillity". In view of the emotive power of Wagner's art and the world-chang-

43

ing Dionysian effects it was capable of inducing *at the expense of reason*, surely the only logical dialectical step in a forward direction can now be a willing renunciation of affective power in favour of technical order in and for itself – an 'order' which might of its very nature obscure the old affective syntax and grammar altogether. We achieve a magical inversion of the old dominance of subjective romantic 'expression' (bound up with tonal *harmony* from Kretschmar's point of view). Such feelings as may now be evoked by a newly objective art of primarily *polyphonic* integrity, will be more or less accidental – a roulette-game of affective content, which, by virtue of its very emancipation from the composer's will, might attain the only sort of 'truth' possible in such matters: a truth beyond parody, gleaming in the gaps between the rigid configurations of an arbitrary but total system. Once again the release of such truth therefore becomes a mystical act – a conjuring with numbers.

In describing this initial span of the idealogical progression which is implied (and often stressed by Zeitblom) to be the background to Leverkühn's creative development in the novel, we have, as it were, accompanied the composer from the parodistic *Ocean Lights*, through the increasing polyphonic rigours of the Brentano settings to the opera *Love's Labour's Lost* (the "clever parody in notes" as of a "music-lover who had tired of romantic democracy and popular moral harangues and demanded an art for art's sake . . ." – a "tense, sustained, neck-breaking game played by art at the edge of impossibility").[9] There follows the orchestral fantasy, *Marvels of the Universe:*

... a sneering travesty of praise which seems to apply not only to the frightful clockwork of the world-structure but also to the medium used to describe it: yes, repeatedly to music itself, the cosmos of sound. The piece has contributed not a little to the reproach levelled at the art of my friend, as a virtuosity antipathetic to the artist mind, a blasphemy, a nihilistic sacrilege.[10]

Obeying the fatal laws of the dialectical process in which he is locked, Leverkühn's parodistic style, born of prodigious perception, has turned to scorn and mockery. His art has unequivocally turned into an almost direct metaphorical equivalent of Jonathan Leverkühn's 'osmotic growths': abortive crystalline imitations of natural forms, which yet "are dead",[11] as the composer's father observed with tears in his eyes.

We should nevertheless recall that for all the lie of their natural, plant-like appearance, these crystalline growths were heliotropic; that they "pathetically" strove towards the sunlight when one side of the aquarium was exposed. One of the things that upsets Zeitblom about the *Marvels of the Universe* fantasy is the extent to which it fails to demonstrate the metaphorically 'heliotropic' tendency of his friend's art which he had certainly found present in the slightly earlier setting of Klopstock's *Spring Festival*, which struck him as indeed "a plea to God, an atonement for sin, a work of *attritio cordis* . . . ".[12] The following and, in a sense, final stage of the dialectical process for Leverkühn is as clearly anticipated here as in the earlier Brentano settings; particularly *Grossmutter Schlangen-köchin*, with its curious echoes of German folk-song:

For it is really the case that this music, wise and true and ever shrewd, here continually and painfully woos the folk-air. The wooing remains unrealized, it is there and not there, sounds fleetingly, echoes, fades into a style musically foreign to it from which after all it constantly seeks to escape. The artistic effect is striking: it appears like a cultural paradox, which by inversion of the natural course of development, where the refined and intellectual grow out of the elementary, the former here plays the role of the original, out of which the simple continually strives to wrest itself free.[13]

This 'heliotropic' aspect of Leverkühn's art and personality increases in significance in the novel proportionately as his own fatally ordained descent into the darkness accelerates. It defines the quality of his tragedy, lingering on in the last high G of a solo cello which concludes his final work, the *Dr Fausti Weheklag*, abiding at the last "as a light in the night"[14] – the night, that is, of supreme anguish and ultimate apocalypse of which this and the earlier oratorio had vouchsafed a vision. This in the end is all that Leverkühn can muster of that "intellectually winged simplicity"[15] he had once praised as the "object and craving of art".[16] Subsequently, and in like spirit (that of Nietzsche's yearning for southern lightness and charm to offset Wagner's northern and ailing weightiness), he admits of a desire that art might once again become "per du" with humanity. His own nearest approach to the latter comes perhaps in the Violin Concerto written for Rudi Schwerdtfeger – the charming but "mediocre" wooer of the composer, whose transient success won him a work (from the man who had foresworn love, we recall) that is in fact described as falling "somewhat out of the frame of Leverkühn's ruthlessly radical and uncompromising work as a whole."[17]

Schwerdtfeger himself interestingly comes close to telling Adrian outright that his greatness owes itself, for all that he may wish, to his very "inhumanity";[18] and on more than one occasion Zeitblom stresses the composer's attendant personal air of aloofness in society, related to his coldness in personal relationships of course, which "gave one the feeling that he came from a country where nobody else lived."[19] This country, one might add, reading Mann's implied analysis to the full, is one where nobody *can* live, save that he strikes a bargain with the Devil, that he assents to the fatal coercion of his will to Dionysian possession that bears fruit in artistic revelation; that he takes on the mantle, that is, of the dying Faust as Artist-Seer – a figure born in the special darkness of the German Middle Ages, of the time of Luther's Reformation. The black joke that Mann has his 'Devil' play upon Leverkühn is that the godlike ecstasy of creation serves a series of great works whose expressive content grows more and more openly distant from transcendent 'godlike ecstasy', being in the end nothing but a revelation of the proper darkness of humanity, of an inner hell of madness and despair, born of the sickness of a civilization. Grasping the dark mantle about his shoulders for longer than any other might dare (with devil-granted strength), Leverkühn plunges on to the logical end of the road of the Faustian Artist, where, in a world gone mad and heading for disaster, his art (and here Mann's analysis joins hands with Adorno's) becomes a case-study of hopelessness. The only hope in the whole sorry affair lies perhaps in that last cello G of the *Fausti Wehe-klag*, or in the Devil's hint at a possible redemption in posterity (and here Mann's Devil may perhaps be seen to share the ambiguous sanction of God granted to Goethe's Mephistopheles in the Prologue in Heaven): "You will lead the way, you will strike up the march of the future, the lads will swear by your name who thanks to your madness will no longer need to be mad."[20]

★ ★ ★

The attraction of venturing away from the central, intellectual problems of Adrian Leverkühn and into the symbolic and metaphysical machinery of the novel is manifestly strong. But it is dangerous, because the wonderful artistic momentum and inevitability of the whole thing charms out of our minds the vital question: Need it have been so?

That I would wish to give a negative answer to this question is no doubt clear. But it is important to be sure about what we are doing in rejecting the apparent inevitability of Leverkühn's inner dialectic. It is certainly not to reject the consistency of this dialectic on its own terms, nor its potency as an analytical statement about twentieth-century Western music. What I would rather do is pay homage to the persuasive validity of Mann's analysis, but suggest at the same time that the creative dialectic whose stages he articulates in those of Leverkühn's development as a composer, takes at one point a turn that is as much arbitrary, and dependent upon an unanalysed historical mood, as altogether 'logical'. And let us be clear that the isolation of this logical quirk in Leverkühn's development casts a suspicious and critical light not upon Mann's hero (in whom a larger ironic purpose must be assumed to be working), so much as upon the whole complex of twentieth-century art in the West. One can hardly suggest that a whole period of creative activity has been simply wrong or misguided, but one can stress the relativism of cultural 'necessities'.

The problematic point in Leverkühn's development to which I have referred is precisely that recorded in his Chapter 15 letter to Wendell Kretschmar (see above, pp. 41–2). I have tried already to demonstrate from within, as it were, the particular logic of the inner dialectic there consciously initiated by Adrian and whose successive stages, as intellectual formulations, will condition the kind of art he subsequently produces. It is emphatically *not* the other way round. Adrian is heir to a line of nineteenth-century German composers who enthroned Beethoven as their God precisely for the way in which his art openly embraced literary techniques and ideas. In the earlier Romantic period philosophers were by nature artists, and thought on the highest level was often thought about art – the generation of ideas that placed the Artist even above the Philosopher. Only towards the end of the century, and in the wake of Wagner, do we clearly see ideas suddenly taking a leap *beyond* art, appearing now (one thinks of a central strain in Nietzsche's thought, more particularly still of Freud) to leave it behind as something 'seen through' and regarded as an activity ripe for outgrowing and discarding upon the banks that edge the road of human destiny – banks upon which, further back, lay the ritual masks of primitive religious practices, the moral codes of ancient communities.

It is surely at just such a juncture of intellectual history that Mann would have us picture Adrian Leverkühn as he allows his insight into the techniques of artistic emotion-fabrication (as he sees it) to lead him to suspect all affective gesture in human intercourse, even the very thing in itself: the emotional affect that such gestures had once been supposed to 'express'. Interestingly, what Mann seems to do here is send Leverkühn off down the post-Wagnerian path whose particular 'logic' we have discussed, while having himself elsewhere planted a signpost pointing in the direction of an alternative route, whose existence he seems not disposed to admit of in the catalogue of fatality that is *Doctor Faustus*. The signpost to which I refer comes specifically, and quite properly, in the form of a counter-cry to one of the central indictments of Wagner made by his post-Nietzschean detractors. For all that it is uttered in the politically 'mined' context of the 1933 essay 'Sufferings and Greatness of Richard Wagner', the point is a serious one and well worth quoting here:

All criticism, even Nietzsche's, tends to attribute the effectiveness of art to a conscious and deliberate intention of the artist, and to suggest calculation. Quite falsely and mistakenly: as though every artist does not do just what he *is*, what seems beautiful and good to *him*; as though there could be a kind of artist to whom his own effectiveness was a sham, instead of being, as it always is, an effect first of all upon him, the artist himself![21]

The artist still, and even more irrevocably perhaps, stands or falls with his work; and Mann says nothing here that would question the validity of any Leverkühnian insight into the workings of the Act III Prelude from *Die Meistersinger*. Nevertheless, this way of looking at the overall phenomenon does unmistakably suggest a different conclusion to be drawn. The old artist-audience formula no longer works in the familiar way. On the highest level we might more properly start with a wholly intimate expressive complex in which the effect of the work is paired with an initial desire for, or readiness to indulge that effect for reasons of the artist's personal experience. Between these two, the working-out, the realization or 'forming' in artistic objectivity could be said to assume once more its traditional role of means rather than end. In the light of a potentially more modern psychological awareness, the intellectually exorcized affect is simply replaced by an autonomous complex of desire and desired-reaction, which might in the end be regarded as but the old expressive content (as it had drawn to itself the vocabulary of vision and inspiration) examined under a new microscope. Can one really say, as Adrian would appear to do, that the thing in itself has disappeared, registering the knowledge in the self-lacerating scornfulness and the yearning for sincerity that is at the heart of the parody to which he resorts (rather in the way that a child might turn against a doll that he has chanced to see his mother restuffing; the magic seems to have gone – and artists, like children, are sensitive to the desecration of illusion)?

Apart from the heliotropic lamentation of his final cantata, all Adrian's mature work is, as a result of this supposed revelation, post-lapsarian in a particular and tragic way: fatally, hypersensitively aware of itself and its own processes, of, in a deeper sense, its own futility. Art, the way of life of childhood, both racial and personal, had found its particular innocence celebrated and conceptually justified in the West by the wilful un-knowing of the Church-dominated Middle Ages, by the reverence for man of classical antiquity and the Renaissance, even of the reason-obsessed Enlightenment. Recurring puritanical rejection of it by the Church simply served to reinforce intuitive awe of its power. Only the spirit of modern science and, paradoxically, Romanticism itself seem to have combined to ignite the logs about Valhalla, where the Artist-Gods – all too aware of their misdeeds and of the wilful subterfuge by which they have sought to conceal them – await their downfall.

Of course, they were indeed personally to blame for much, but is not the whole apocalyptic vision dispersed by simply admitting that they had never been Gods at all? Might we not suggest to Adorno, apropos of his undoubtedly brilliant analysis in the *Philosophy of Modern Music*, that art had in a sense always and only been 'case-study', while Schoenberg's art in fact, through horror at the realization, *ceased* to be such: turning (in *Erwartung*, for example) into the self-conscious model of a case-study, based on the literary and scientific ideas of his day, that has absolutely no value *as* a case-study for that very reason? It becomes merely a marginal illustration to the work of Freud who, like the character in Schoenberg's opera (not Schoenberg himself), speaks in a language we understand of whatever undiscovered country; the language of compassion and excitement, of horror and despair.

In Leverkühn, as in Schoenberg and, to a slightly different degree, in Stravinsky, what we really see is the final victory of the word and the idea over music. Leverkühn 'takes back' Beethoven's Ninth in more ways than he himself perhaps realized – but it is a victory that simply need not have been won. Indeed, I would put it that had nineteenth-century German thought not woven a culturally established Music and a conceptually protean Nature so persuasively together, and had the very particular kind of anti-Wagnerism in the works of Gustav Mahler, that great Wagnerian musician, or even the later Richard Strauss, been fully understood by his contemporaries, then twentieth-century music, perhaps twentieth-century art as a whole, might have taken a course different from the one it did. But such speculation is irrelevant. Certainly had Adrian Leverkühn understood Mahler, his fate could (I do not say would) have been different.

FOUR

Adorno's *Philosophy of Modern Music*

*Today art in its entirety, and music in partic-
ular, feels the shattering effects of that very
process of enlightenment in which it participates
and upon which its own progress depends.*[1]

Much of the most accessible writing on twentieth-
century music has the air of preaching to the con-
verted. The dogmas are simplified, the history of their
adherents is charted, but the problems and doubts of
the unbeliever remain – their strength depending upon
the extent to which he is prepared to hold out against
the so-convincing commitment of those who have
'seen'. It is the great failing of modern musical criticism that it has signally scorned the building of bridges
between the common man (in all of us) and the
singular artist ploughing his lonely path into heaven
knows what realms of arcane experience. There are
signs that the young are already happier to shrug off
the whole central-European 'modernist' movement

(stretching from the death of Mahler into the 1950s, although late manifestations still thrive in cultural glass-houses) rather than grapple with the quirky exegesis of prophets who appear not to comprehend unbelief.

The dangers of facile regression have haunted Faustian, Western culture since the Renaissance; a culture that has worthily feared the doom of reliving misunderstood history, whatever ironic Fate might actually decree. It is precisely in the spirit of this tradition, and in recognition that modernism was indeed a movement of thought and experience (with a clear, if hell-bent, inner logic) that I would turn to Theodor Adorno, as did Thomas Mann in the 1940s, for illumination of its dark world, and particularly of its central *fons et origo*, Arnold Schoenberg.

* * *

I believe Adorno's *Philosophy of Modern Music* (1948) to be one of the most penetrating and profound of the few critical works (amongst which we might include Mann's *Doctor Faustus*) to offer the kind of illumination that I have suggested to be seriously lacking in the majority of modernist apologias. For all that the impossibility of linking the general with the specific is a theme in his book, that is precisely what it manages to do, in the sense that it provides a comprehensible explanation of the significance of the phenomenon while in no way denying what one might call the common-sense reaction to it. Instead of restricting his discussion to questions of technique and stylistic 'necessity', and thus begging the question "Why?", Adorno accepts the commonsense reaction of one unfamiliar with such things to a work of Schoenberg's middle or late period. Indeed it *is* strange and even incomprehensible, he effectively observes, but this strange incomprehensibility is part of its very essence and significance.

One must work at Adorno, however. His great misfortune is that his written style presents a surface as hermetic, as protective of its esoteric content and lacking in "loop-holes" as the ultra-progressive musical works with which his discussion largely deals. Yet whereas close and prolonged study of Schoenberg's *Wind Quintet* may achieve its reward in a quaint familiarity with the inexplicable that overrides the original search for comprehension of its content, careful and patient reading of Adorno will indeed reveal a content of remarkable quality – for all that we may come to understand the central epithet in Mann's description of him as "uncompromising, tragically brilliant, operating on the highest level."[2]

The *Philosophy of Modern Music* takes the form of a pair of long essays dealing with Schoenberg and Stravinsky respectively. The Stravinsky essay ('Stravinsky and Restoration') is the shorter of the two, and was conceived specifically to round out the nevertheless comprehensive view of modern music incorporated into 'Schoenberg and Progress', which had been written seven years previously as an independent study. Adorno saw the two figures as representing necessarily linked, yet diametrically opposed, aspects of musical modernism in the West, but it is vital to point out here that while the Schoenberg essay charts the however tragic career of an heroic progressive, the Stravinsky essay has something of the character of a polemical attack on a wily, and even inhuman regressive.

It is the Schoenberg essay that forms the backbone of the book, however, and which I shall attempt to explain in the fashion of an exegesis of its argument. First, some background on Adorno himself is necessary. For in a sense he is an even more total and signal product of precisely that tradition in which he locates Schoenberg: the Faustian tradition of German music from Beethoven through to Mahler that had been dominated by ideas since its early involvement with the development of Romantic literature, to the extent that in Schoenberg it almost becomes pure idea – the act of composition an almost irrelevant example and extension of thought about the very possibility of artistic expression. It might almost be that Adorno's essay on Schoenberg is to be regarded as a work *within* that tradition as important as any of Schoenberg's compositions. I quote further from Mann's biographical sketch of Adorno:

> ... born in 1903 in Frankfurt-am-Main. His father was a German Jew; his mother, herself a singer, was the daughter of a French army officer of Corsican – originally Genoese – descent and of a German singer.... Having grown up in an atmosphere entirely dominated by theory (politi-

cal theory as well) and artistic, primarily musical interests, he studied philosophy and music. In 1931 he assumed the post of Lecturer at Frankfurt University and taught philosophy there until he was expelled by the Nazis. Since 1941 he has been living in Los Angeles; . . .

All his life this remarkable man has refused to choose between the professions of philosophy and music. He felt that he was actually pursuing the same thing in both divergent realms. His dialectic turn of mind and bent towards social history is interlinked with a passion for music. The phenomenon is no longer unique nowadays and is doubtless connected with the whole complex of problems of our time. In pursuit of this passion, he studied composition and piano, at first with music instructors in Frankfurt, then with Alban Berg and Eduard Steuermann in Vienna. From 1928 to 1931 he was editor of the Vienna *Anbruch*, and was active in promoting radical modern music.[3]

*   *   *

It is not necessary – nor am I qualified to do so – to deal here with Adorno's intellectual relationship with Horkheimer or with the particular philosophical programme of the so-called Frankfurt School, which they led, and their work in the Institute for Social Research. For all that its sociological and philosophical jargon contributes to the density of its surface (and its musical references depend upon a broadly comprehensive knowledge of the output of the Second

Viennese School and much else in the way of twentieth-century and earlier music), comprehension of the *Philosophy of Modern Music* depends considerably upon the will not to be dissuaded by the range of its references, but to stretch out the elliptically compressed sentences until they yield the nugget of meaning that must then be placed within the broader developing framework of the argument. For the argument *does* develop, in spite of the fact that it frequently appears to progress in as confusingly circular a fashion as the path followed by the lonely demented woman through the forest in Schoenberg's *Erwartung*. One influence in particular is crucial here: that of Hegel, quotations from whom head major sections of the book. A vital key to the structure of 'Schoenberg and Progress' is to be found in the form of the Hegelian 'dialectic'. Following the subsequently added general Introduction, we have a three-part discussion which in Hegelian terminology follows the pattern: *Thesis* (from the section entitled 'Disturbance of the Work' to 'Expressionism as Objectivity'), *Antithesis* (from 'Total Organization of the Elements of Music' to 'Form') and *Synthesis* (from 'The Composers' to 'Attitude towards Society'). More conventionally we might describe these three sections as (1) the case for Schoenberg's particular kind of 'progress' – its inner consistency and social 'truth' explained; (2) a critique of Schoenberg's inconsistencies and analysis of his particular kind of 'failure'; (3) an extended conclusion in which a more comprehensive case is made out for Schoenberg, one that includes the negative aspects isolated in the second section. I will discuss each of these three sections in order.

* * *

The hero, or would-be hero of Adorno's tale is to be the Progressive Artist. While it soon becomes clear that such a figure is more or less embodied in the actual person of Arnold Schoenberg, it is important to understand this figure as a complex of resonant ideas. Progress involves change (the concepts of artistic innovation and originality are involved here). In that all change in art depends to some extent – positively or negatively, self-consciously or intuitively – upon an attitude adopted to the culturally determined products that were available to the nascent artist, then in all art, according to its relative acquiescence to or rejection of tradition, we have that stance which Adorno sees as essentially a 'philosophical' one. On the highest level of self-consciousness the innovative artist, who rejects certain aspects of the 'tradition', also and inevitably rejects certain aspects of the society that had fostered and supported that tradition. Extending logically from the Faustian, Germanic tradition of the artist as having become more and more an 'outsider' in bourgeois society, and depending upon Adorno's own, in part Marxist-inspired dissatisfaction with the repressive society of modern mass-production, his ideal Progressive Artist becomes one who rejects all that hampers or in any way taints his personal freedom and individualism. All clichés are to be examined, all popular-art-inspired sentimentality and lazy thinking is to be rejected. And the intellectual element is crucial. For Adorno makes no bones about the fact that the artist is essentially far more than a mere craftsman or solipsistic pattern-maker. Art is central to the progress of human enlightenment "in which it participates and upon which its own progress depends".

Adorno's Artist-Hero is still Mahler's: one who through the very truthfulness of expression would answer the questions of the sphinx-riddler who is 'Nature' or 'the World' or 'Fate'. There is also no question that the old Romantic notion of the importance of subjective truth applies in a special sense: for the enlightenment of which we have spoken depends surely enough upon the artist's first duty to find and define an image of *himself* which corresponds most comprehensively to the 'truth' that he feels within himself. In art above all are the larger questions and the particular image seen to be related in curious fashion. It is precisely concern at the immense influential and coercive power of modern mass culture, with its mass-produced 'arts' that leads Adorno to whip his image of the Progressive Artist into one whose first and foremost task becomes the relentless and even systematic purification of his 'language' of all that is imposed from without by tradition and society.

Social truth must be pursued in opposition to a society that begins to take on the mythological properties of a repressive father. His every taste and mannerism must be ruthlessly expunged from within himself by the son who would seek his own truth and freedom. Is it significant, indeed, that Adorno, whose patronymic was Wiesengrund, should have adopted his mother's maiden name? A Freudian as much as he was a Hegelian, Adorno might well have accepted this point, although in the confusing configuration of *personal* (perhaps psychological?) and *social* truth Adorno chooses to regard the latter as of primary concern, and thus presents us with his ideal artist as one who is justifiably engaged in the task of "concrete negation".

What is so remarkable about Adorno's concept of the progressive is that, whether we read the projected analysis in sociological or psychological terms, it appears to fit the reality of Schoenberg's middle phase like a glove, accommodating (as I have indicated) the 'commonsense' reaction to his music in a vital and positive consideration of its significance. Thus where the standard critical explanation of Schoenberg's middle period may speak of the previously impending 'collapse' of post-Tristanesque chromatic tonality and of the so-called 'free atonality' of the Five Orchestral Pieces (op. 16) or *Erwartung*, Adorno makes it quite clear that we are dealing with consciously attained expressive effects here. Rather than fixing his sights rigidly upon the stylistic surface of these works, Adorno attempts to account for their nature as the products of a quest for expressive truth that avoids at every point the clichés and gestures of extension, of climax and release, that have become comfortable and pleasant precisely because they gratify and assuage to an extent that no longer corresponds to the artist's inner sense of the truth of the matter. *Tristan* may express the agony of yearning (and so on), but how alluring and consumable is this music that Wagner himself was happy to be "engulfed in". Ever pressed by the gratification-hungry bourgeois audience (here the coercion of society begins to express itself in the form of cultural acceptance and success), the composer may indulge in these gestures and mannerisms of post-Romantic subjectivity to the point where they are in truth as synthetic and stylized as the affective formulae of the Baroque. Hence Adorno observes of Schoenberg:

> The actual revolutionary moment for him is the change in function of musical expression. Passions are no longer simulated, but rather genuine emotions of the unconscious – of shock, of trauma – are registered without disguise through the medium of music. . . . The first atonal works are case-studies [*Protokolle*] in the sense of psychoanalytic dream case-studies.[4]

This reading of the situation helps us to see that it was not musical language in the later nineteenth century that was disintegrating so much as musical form. In a relatively progressive 'late' composer such as Mahler (as he might appear in Adorno's mythology) the increasing extension of the formal unit is constantly at war with the eruptive power of the moment of expression. In Schoenberg these moments fully destroy even the possibility of a form, which can only imply an order that is imposed, whether we consider such form desirable or 'natural' ('Nature' in Adorno is always to be understood as with inverted commas, as but a convenient fabrication). The progressive composer, in his quest for total freedom of 'true' expression, must rigorously avoid regression to the womb of set forms, as he must avoid the "impotent clichés" of traditional sounds. Of course, the very fact that Schoenberg was still producing extended works suggests that a kind of form is present which the progressive apologist must account for; and this Adorno does by developing the notion that Schoenberg's later formal moulds, rather than being imposed from outside, are derived from the very nature of the expressionistic gesture. His description of *Erwartung* is central to his argument at this point:

> ... *Erwartung* has as its heroine a woman looking for her lover at night. She is subjected to all the terrors of darkness and in the end comes upon his murdered corpse. She is consigned to music in the very same way as a patient is to analysis. The admission of hatred and desire, jealousy and forgiveness, and – beyond all this – the entire symbolism of the unconscious is wrung from her; it is only in the moment that the heroine becomes insane that the music recalls its right to utter a consoling protest. The seismographic registration of traumatic shock becomes, at the same time, the technical structural law of music. It forbids continuity and development. Musical language is polarized according to its extremes: towards gestures of shock resembling bodily convulsions on the one hand, and on the other towards a crystalline standstill of a human being whom anxiety causes to freeze in her tracks. It is this polarization upon which the total world of form of the mature Schoenberg – and of Webern as well – depends.[5]

★ ★ ★

It should be just at this point that we begin to ask questions: Is Truth, then, solely to be sought in the Freudian unconscious? Does not the very precision with which Schoenberg has fabricated a musical model of this same wayward and distraught unconscious, preclude our using his works as *material* for a 'case-study'? (Are these gestures not conditioned by the very *idea* of the Freudian unconscious, as Wagner's by the bourgeois desire for gratification and reward?) Is not the "compositional will" of the reactionary and conventional composer, however socially, culturally or psychologically determined, also a kind of 'truth'? Can we not conceive of an alternative line of 'progress' that involves rather the suspicion that the very model of the artist, as one who must seek in 'freedom' a totally unconditioned and specific inner truth, is based on a fundamental misconception? It is also at this point, however (and herein lies the great quality of his essay) that Adorno begins to acknowledge and even answer some of these very questions in a manner that not surprisingly upset Schoenberg, who never did grasp that the *Philosophy of Modern Music* was on *his* side at the expense of Stravinsky.[6]

The climax of Adorno's exegesis of the heroic 'logic' of Schoenberg's compositional development comes with his extension of the idea that in *Erwartung* the "registration of traumatic shock becomes ... the technical structural law of music". The development of twelve-tone composition is now accommodated as a means whereby all influences on the manner of compositional extension are systematically eliminated. Correctness of organization becomes the sole criterion.

The very "dream of subjectivity"[7] having finally exploded, Schoenberg fashions a kind of work that has nothing to do with the illusory shapes of conflict and resolution, tension and climax. Having no 'high points', Schoenberg's ideal serial work is "equidistant in all its moments from a central point": "Music formulates a design of the world, which – for better or worse – no longer recognizes history."[8]

Already, however, we are moving into that section of Adorno's argument which I have described as Antithesis. The curious nature of our Progressive Artist's goal can no more avoid the commonsense observer than the nightmare images of the middle period. Structure has now clearly "to be correct rather than meaningful". 'Nature' has been dominated for the sake of a number-game that relates to astrology: "Twelve-tone rationality approaches superstition *per se* in that it is a closed system – one which is opaque even unto itself – in which the configuration of means is directly hypostatized as goal and as law."[9] If the goal of Schoenberg's later career is to find a meaning in the organization, then Adorno finds the intention mocked, almost allegorically, "in an emptiness which extends into the innermost cells of the work of art."[10] If the heroically dominated bourgeois 'nature' is to be associated with the concept of 'fate', then has not fate reduplicated itself in these works that have no room for meaning?

> Twelve-tone technique is truly the fate of music. It enchains music by liberating it. . . . The subject subordinates itself to this blind nature, seeking protection and security, which it indicates in its

despair over the impossibility of fulfilling music out of itself. . . . Liberated music seeks to reconstitute the lost totality – the lost power and the responsibly binding force of Beethoven. Music succeeds in so doing only at the price of its freedom, and thereby it fails.[11]

It is impossible to avoid the sad truth that the self-determined work has become repressive in nature. Progressive truth is lost when the system becomes normative and the ironic fact emerges that the escape from all social pressure has produced a music which reduplicates it: "The force to which man is subjected by mass-music continues to live on as a socially opposite pole in that music which totally withdraws from man."[12]

The apologia has become the record of a tragedy. With ruthless logic Adorno goes on to detail the "coarsening"[13] effects of the serial levelling of musical language: nuances are lost, a special kind of monotony arises; pseudo-classical forms are reverted to, yet they have only the characteristics of "the death-masks of the profiles of instrumental music", which are "impotent and noncommittal".[14] An overriding arbitrariness takes over in this fatally static music – fatal "because all dynamics come to a standstill within it without finding release".[15]

Discussing Schoenberg's later style of orchestration, Adorno likens the effect to that of a great machine in which everything whirrs and flies round at great speed and which yet remains rooted to the spot. The dream-like case-study of the middle period has now unequivocally become no more than "the hypothesis of a case-study".[16] While some hope might be found in the "limited subjectivity"[17] of Schoenberg's late works ("The truly great moments in late Schoenberg have been attained despite the twelve-tone technique as well as by means of it ..."[18]), the composer fails to settle the dispute between this limited subjectivity and "alienated objectivity".[19] The technique born of a quest for transcendent freedom has become an instrument of finally coercive power: "For the very sake of its blind unique law this technique denies itself expression, transposing it into the sphere of past memories, thinking to find there the dream-image of the future...."[20]

★ ★ ★

These are harsh and squarely-hitting criticisms. Of that there must be no doubt. Yet if at the end of this central section of his essay we consider ourselves justified in feeling able to dispense with Schoenberg with a knowing smile, we will shortly find ourselves to have been mistaken. The analysis initially appears clear. Schoenberg's particular kind of truth has been achieved "at a very high cost".[21] His new "language of absolute alienation"[22] is one that madly requires the user "to create a unique vocabulary and syntax for every sentence he writes":[23]

Rattling idiotic systems lie in wait to devour any composer who might innocently pretend that this self-invented language had already found confirmation. The fact that the subject does not grow with them makes these difficulties all the more disastrous. The atomization of fragmentary musical moments, presumed by the self-made language, closely parallels the state of the subject. It is broken by total impotence.[24]

We nevertheless begin to approach the particular synthesis that Adorno achieves in the concluding sections of his essay, with the warning that shortly follows:

No artist is able to overcome, through his own individual resources, the contradiction of enchained art within an enchained society. The most which he can hope to accomplish is the contradiction of such a society through emancipated art, and even in this attempt he might well be the victim of despair.[25]

One of the most seriously demanding of Adorno's concluding points is that to care for truth and freedom must be to realize that there is no viable alternative in our society, on the level of high art, to the grim predicament of Schoenberg's final phase. In the context of the Second Viennese School, Webern simply "realizes twelve-tone technique and thus no longer composes: silence is the rest of his mastery".[26] Berg, on the other hand, composes twelve-tone music that seeks to hide its own identity and achieves a "premature reconciliation".[27] Yet Berg's weakness is that "he can renounce nothing at his disposal, whereas the power of all new music lies precisely in renunciation".[28] For all the "intense inner beauty of Berg's late works",[29] Adorno feels compelled to observe that "Schoenberg's inhuman coldness is superior to Berg's magnanimous warmth".[30]

How are we to understand or sympathize with this extraordinary statement? In the subsequent essay's attack on Stravinsky – precisely for the inhumanity of his systematic regression and machine-inspired "dehumanization" of music (he is subsequently consigned to the role of a peripheral phenomenon for the reason that he "avoids the dialectical confrontation with the musical progress of time"[31]) – we should be able to find evidence in plenty that Adorno's case in no way rested on the vindictive animus of some new barbarism. Quite the reverse. A curiously elevated compassion animates Adorno's concluding pronouncements, as he ponders the sad truth that the "possibility of music itself has become uncertain"[32] not so much through the corrupting influence of decadent individualism as its reverse! Real progress might now be envisaged only through *emancipation* from the twelve-tone system, but this darkness is something which can be transcended only through experience; there can be no evasion.

For all the manifest failings of Schoenberg's twelve-tone compositions, they have at least successfully resisted every gratification-impulse and 'untruth' of mass society (and are consequently hated by the very bourgeois audience to which they quite properly belong as the ultimate image of its own brutal impotence). They have attained to a new freedom, yet "It is precisely for this freedom that music is being trained by twelve-tone technique – not so much by means of what the technique determines in compositions, but rather through what is prohibited by it."[33] Describing this same technique as a "merciless samaritan",[34]

Adorno shortly goes on to suggest that it is now precisely concerned "with the handing-down of technical standards in the face of impending barbarism".[35]

We are now in a position where we might understand Adorno's earlier, resonant suggestion about these same twelve-tone compositions: "Whatever escapes from the impending ice age might well survive in their labyrinth."[36] In the face of all that it now no longer feels it can 'say' with any truth or justification, the work of art has submerged the subject and become hermetically sealed into an aesthetic object without loopholes. It can no longer think but merely be the object of thought. Its surface, would we but understand it, reflects the meaningless aspect of a "meaningless world",[37] and such light as it sheds upon this world is produced in a self-sacrificial effort: "It has taken upon itself all the darkness and guilt of the world. Its fortune lies in the perception of misfortune; all of its beauty is in denying itself the illusion of beauty."[38]

Such consolation as is finally to be derived from Adorno is summed up in the grim pronouncement: "The inhumanity of art must triumph over the inhumanity of the world for the sake of the humane."[39] Simply by hanging on doggedly to the image of a reality that can only be expressed as a "concrete negation", Adorno's Progressive Artist stakes his all upon the image of a new man in a Utopian society who will redeem his suffering by having been born of it. The ironic tragedy, however, must be that this same artist has necessarily all but opted out of the culture that alone can provide the soil in which his seed might grow and bear fruit. The closing observation of Adorno's essay is as follows:

> No one wishes to become involved with art – individuals as little as collectives. It dies away unheard, without even an echo. If time crystall-ises around that music which has been heard, revealing its radiant quintessence, music which has not been heard falls into empty space like an impotent bullet. Modern music spontaneously aims towards this last experience, evidenced hourly in mechanical music. Modern music sees absolute oblivion as its goal. It is the surviving message of despair from the shipwrecked [*Sie ist die wahre Flaschenpost*].[40]

★ ★ ★

The stark beauty of Adorno's vision in this essay is a moving tribute to the life's work of a difficult and curious man – paradoxically even the only such tribute that convincingly underlines Schoenberg's often expressed opinion about his own importance. It is convincing precisely because it eschews the evasive fetishism of the vast body of Schoenberg literature (inspired and even dominated by Schoenberg's own writings, writings that Adorno not surprisingly finds himself able to quote from on only one or two isolated occasions) – a fetishism, that is, with the question of compositional techniques that Adorno himself saw as one of the unfortunate legacies of the twelve-tone revolution. Perhaps referring directly to Schoenberg's own writings and teaching activities, Adorno had observed:

> The preponderance of doctrinal teaching offers magnificent proof of the manner in which the developmental tendency of the technique leaves the traditional concept of the work far behind. Productive interest is distracted from the individual composition and concentrated, rather, upon the typical possibilities of composition. This results in the transformation of the composition into nothing more than a mere means for the manufacture of the pure language of music.[41]

The achievement of 'Schoenberg and Progress' – and by extension the whole *Philosophy* – is that it retrieves modern music for humanity through a deeply committed exercise in humane criticism that both sets a high standard as such and revitalizes our almost lost belief in the importance of the artist in Western cultural experience. To see Schoenberg as a tragically, even heroically necessary, *failure* may prove paradoxically to grant him that very place of importance in the history of Western music that he clearly believed himself to occupy. It may be that his compositional career can be shown to have been determined by a complex of purely local intellectual and psychological confusions, yet by supplying the idea that had been so confusingly veiled and even directly denied by the Schoenberg style, Adorno provides us with an invaluable tool for analysing and putting into perspective what we might call the Schoenberg phenomenon, whose cultural actuality and persistent legacy can in no sense be denied.

It may be that we should do well to see both the composer and his apologist as equally tragically determined and limited by that very German tradition from whose central stock they both stemmed. I cannot, however, conceive of any attempt at a revaluation of the alternative traditions and specific figures that Adorno, implicitly or explicitly, consigns to the periphery of the great march of the 'dialectic of enlightenment', which avoided confrontation with the argument of the *Philosophy*. Adorno has perhaps fulfilled the role of the first explorer of an unknown sea to bring back a map of its islands and land-masses. The proportions may be wrong and its detailed features may need to be rearranged. It could nevertheless prove the only really useful aid available to subsequent cartographers who would steer an even surer course than Adorno between the Scylla of consumer society's trivializing reduction of art to a branch of mass diversion and the Charybdis of the belief that the gates of Parnassus are rusted shut for ever.

FIVE

An Essay by Schoenberg

Arnold Schoenberg was a strange man. A mass of odd contradictions and queer promptings lurk in the shadow of his heroic image as Scott-of-the-Antarctic of modern music. His importance and even greatness are on a certain level indisputable, but their precise extent relates far more clearly than is often understood to the dimensions of this shadow, which falls nowhere more strikingly than across his writings.

The considerable extent to which Schoenberg was self-taught in basic musical skills undoubtedly contributed to the aptitude he demonstrated for presenting theoretical material in an original and thorough manner. From the *Harmonielehre* of 1911 to the late American textbooks on composition and counterpoint, the radical composer produced a collection of musical-theoretical studies that began to develop a reputation as canonic works amongst academics in the decades following his death. Amusingly, where his compositions would originally have been excluded, the theoretical works were much more readily absorbed by an academic establishment that warmed, for unexamined reasons of its own, to Schoenberg's reverence for the Great Tradition of German music in which he was so concerned to locate himself. Almost in spite of themselves, the academicians found themselves forced by the alluring ring of Schoenberg's rehearsal of the old arguments about the proper logic of historical development and progress to admit the once-offending compositions. They were no more liked, but could suddenly be seen to be comfortingly explainable in terms of the very tradition they had once seemed to undermine. A new race of university composers and 'modern music' specialists was nurtured on Schoenberg texts like the essay 'Brahms the Progressive', in the belief that reverence for the masters, organic development and elliptical phraseology (somehow linked with 'inspiration') together formed the comprehensible bridge between the Old and the New. It is significant that they should have found little to remark on with respect to the extraordinary ideology of that essay, in whose second section this surprising statement appears: "An artist need not think very much, if only he thinks correctly and straight-forwardly."[1]

What, one might nervously enquire, constitutes 'correct thinking' for the straightforward artist? Does it not at least merit comment that Schoenberg, that most intellectual and unstraightforward of composers, working within a tradition in which the creative and the intellectual were considered to be converging pursuits, should devote so many words to fostering an attitude that was ostensibly anti-words, even anti-intellectual? Are we really to believe that in the end it is only a question of rules and inspiration after all, or does the mask of Schoenberg, the romantically-inclined, authoritarian conservative, conceal a more private face in whose expression the iconoclastic radical can be discerned? It is my contention that Schoenberg's writings merit the closest critical scrutiny, for reasons that can best be demonstrated in the context of an essay that takes the form of an apparently sincere, even humbled reappraisal of a composer to whom he felt he had been unjust.

I refer to the essay entitled simply 'Gustav Mahler' (1912, revised 1948) which appeared as the second item in the collection that was published by Dika Newlin as *Style and Idea* in 1950. The critical substance of this public revaluation of Schoenberg's one-time friend and champion can be summarized without too much difficulty. Starting with the admission that he, like many others, had once distrusted the effect that Mahler's music undoubtedly had upon him (did Mahler, perhaps, deal only in effects for their own sake?), Schoenberg advocates examination of this very unwillingness to be moved. If we trust ourselves and our culture, he suggests, we should be prepared to be "overwhelmed"[2] and not tie ourselves up in the knots of a quibbling intellect. Nevertheless, an intellectual culture requires intellectual justifications, and for this reason we must admit the necessity to split hairs about matters that we might have preferred to consign to the realms of mystery.

The standard criticisms of Mahler's works are now laid before us in more detail, beginning with the charge that they are over-long and possessed of inflated aims that the composer lacked the strength to realize. This Schoenberg considers to be "one of those thoughtless clichés which must be hated above all because they are almost without exception applied to those men to whom they are least appropriate."[3] He goes on to question what such a criticism could possibly refer to. Surprisingly, he answers the question, suggesting that if, after all, it was applied to the works' apparent programmatic content, to Mahler's metaphysical and philosophical concerns, it would have some justification. But many composers of earlier times, Schoenberg reminds us, aspired to seek or to serve 'God'. High aspiration is a quality that need not be defined in terms of specific goals. On the contrary, "there is only one great goal towards which the artist strives: *to express himself*".[4] Everything else, Schoenberg emphasizes, is unimportant: "for everything else is included in it: death, resurrection, Faust, fate – but also the lesser and yet not the less important moments, the emotions of the soul and spirit which make a man creative."[5]

Allowing us little time in which to take in the full implications of this statement, Schoenberg moves on to what he clearly considers potentially more significant accusations: that Mahler's music is prey to both sentimentality and banality. Without pausing for a definition of these terms, we are given to understand that Mahler's themes *do* in fact sound banal; but where a lesser composer might have overcome this by clever manipulation of the notes until the same theme sounded 'clever', Mahler scores by virtue of the fact that his banal-sounding themes can be shown, upon analysis, in fact to have been constructed with great artfulness. The main theme of the Andante of the Sixth Symphony is examined accordingly, its elliptical shortening of the expected number of measures combined with unexpected extension being singled out for praise. To the underlying originality of Mahler's themes, Schoenberg then adds the "almost unexampled objectivity"[6] of his orchestration. He goes on to suggest that his stature as a conductor likewise depended upon single-minded mastery, while his penetrating mind was able to bestow clarity on all that it attended to ("I should even have liked to observe how Mahler knotted his tie. . . ."[7]). Schoenberg's final accolade, however, depends upon the observation that Mahler's career as a composer represented an "uninterrupted ascent",[8] passing through the "tautness and compactness of the form of the Sixth"[9] to a final assault upon the inexpressible, manifested with almost mythical aptness in the fact that the "objective, almost passionless statements"[10] of the Ninth Symphony lead only to the mute riddle of the Tenth, that remains (like Beethoven's) unfinished:

> It seems as if something might be imparted to us in the Tenth which we ought not yet to know, for which we are not yet ready. Those who have written a Ninth stood too near to the hereafter. Perhaps the riddles of this world would be solved, if one of those who knew them were to write a Tenth. And that probably is not to take place.[11]

★   ★   ★

Even presented in this skeletal fashion (I have omitted much additional material to which I will shortly turn), this is an odd testimonial. The list of Mahler's supposed faults contrives to have greater defintion than Schoenberg's rather vacuous critical case on his behalf, for all the exclamation-marks and polemical rumblings that are directed at the erring critics. How convincing *is* this case? Tossed aside as mere irrelevancies are all those profound spiritual and philosophical concerns that the most cursory student of the composer would have to accept as vital determining features of Mahler's artistic personality. In their place Schoenberg serves us up with what sound rather like neoromantic platitudes about "self-expression" and "objectivity". As to what is being expressed or what the 'object' might be we seem at first to be left in the dark – for all that the critical manner grows ostentatiously rigorous, to the extent of including a few pages of thematic analysis. In the end we are left bludgeoned by an enthusiastic devotion to mystical aspiration for the ineffable (it erupts at numerous points throughout the essay) that even the most other-worldly of early nineteenth-century romantics might have found unsubtle.

In fairness we would have to observe that the entire essay has really very little to do with Mahler; I might even venture to doubt that Schoenberg cared a great deal for his works. Like many of his other critical essays, this one seems to have been conceived to some extent as an example of how he would best have liked his own adherents and acolytes to write about himself, and in this the plea for willing submission to the artist's effects should be placed alongside Schoenberg's rueful cry of 1947: "There is nothing I long for more intensely than to be taken for a better sort of Tchaikovsky ... that people should know my tunes and whistle them."[12] The specific case made out for Mahler in this essay comprises only a part of its content, and by no means the most remarkable part. I have observed that advocacy for an aspiration after the mystically inexpressible constantly animates the argument. It forms in fact a major component in the curious substratum of ideas and beliefs, articulated in the form of a covertly expressed credo, which merits the closest consideration.

The expostulatory tone of the very opening page is significantly related to its content. Schoenberg's concern here is for the proper religious fervour of the apostle who would communicate his belief "that Gustav Mahler was one of the greatest men and artists".[13] The extraordinary second paragraph concludes as follows:

> An apostle who does not glow preaches heresy. He to whom the halo of sanctity is denied does not carry the image of a god within himself. For the apostle does not shine by himself, but by a light which uses his body merely as a shell; the light pierces the shell, but it graciously grants the glowing one the appearance of shining by himself. We, who are inspired, must have faith; men will sympathize with this ardour, men will see our light shining. Men will honour the one whom we worship – even without our doing anything about it.[14]

Much is revealed here. Casting himself in the role of

preaching apostle, Schoenberg observes that such a one burns with an albeit reflected light, yet must himself (whether initially or in consequence is not clear) possess the "halo of sanctity". Self-abasement not infrequently betrays itself as the mannerism of self-aggrandizement in Schoenberg's writings, and the strangeness of these thoughts is hardly mitigated by the fact that anyone familiar with the opera *Moses und Aron* will see here almost a preliminary sketch for its conceptual scenario.[15] The later refinement of the composer's mystical notions required the splitting of the burning apostle into the complementary figures of the divinely inspired Moses and the more theatrically 'glowing' Aron respectively. The following statement: "We do not believe enough in the whole thing, in the great thing, but demand irrefutable details"[16] even gives us to understand that the split has already occurred, and that here Schoenberg will act the demonstrative Aron, for all that "The more exactly we observe, the more enigmatic does the simplest matter become to us."[17]

It is difficult to escape the indication in what follows that the particular example of artistic self-expression that Schoenberg is to observe and preach on behalf of is linked in his mind with nature, with an expression of "what is natural".[18] The natural and the miraculous, however, necessarily overlap for Schoenberg the mystic theologian, and to extol the natural is equally to praise the miraculous. He is prepared to play the explaining and justifying Aron only because of the fallen state of intellectual man, who insists on questioning the inspired Moses, who would simply burn with the fire of revelation.

AN ESSAY BY SCHOENBERG

We are to understand, therefore, that Art and Nature coincide in essence as a form of revelation. For all Schoenberg's subsequent emphasis on the nature of art as self-expression, he gives us to understand that this revelation is not simply of subjective human weaknesses (such as are displayed in the "too cheap, too accessible"[19] effects of Puccini). Quite consistently, Schoenberg is shortly speaking openly of "divine works"[20] which must by their very nature be impervious to our merely human comprehension. All we can do, in the fruitless effort to fathom their laws, is to impose our own limited intellectual concepts upon something which is essentially superhuman.

* * *

It will be clear by now into what strange territory we have strayed. A critical revaluation has turned into a homily on the divine nature of the great work of art, attested to by professional initiates who should be believed rather than questioned! It is indeed at this point in the argument that Schoenberg holds in abeyance further discussion of the nature of divine revelation and turns his attention once more to the pettiness of the general mêlée of cultural activity, of the "throng of little men"[21] whose publicity industry typically rejects "the solitary great man"[22] who must flee the mediocre present for a distant, comprehending future. Schoenberg's remaining problem, however, is to tell us something tangibly sympathetic about greatness; something which will bridge the conceptual gulf be-

tween his faith in self-expression as the goal of the
artist and belief in the divinely transcendent rather
than subjectively 'sentimental' content of the Great
Work. Here at last he finds himself in the position
where he must moderate his apostolic ardour to the
extent of giving us discreetly to understand that
Mahler and his Ideal Artist do not in fact coincide
with each other. Self-expression must, in the greatest
works, be something pure and outside the merely
human. The nature of Mahler's self-expression, on the
contrary, is seen to depend upon an ever more nearly
realized *aspiration* for the expression of the necessarily
inexpressible. The feeling that Mahler undoubtedly
expresses redeems itself from mere sentimentality only
by virtue of the remarkable fact that his *true* sorrow
"elevates itself to resignation".[23]

At first this seems a perverse notion, whose precise
meaning is unclear. However, we shortly find ourselves back on the central path of Schoenberg's briefly
interrupted discussion of mystical revelation, when the
nature of this 'resignation' is clarified with respect to
its moments of attainment in the Sixth Symphony.
The "sorrow-torn upheaval" of its first movement, we
are told,

> generates its opposite, the unearthly passage with
> the cowbells, whose cool, icy comfort is bestowed
> from a height which is reached only by one who
> soars to resignation; only he can hear it who
> understands what heavenly voices whisper
> without animal warmth.[24]

Here we have it. In yet another latterday version of the
renunciation of the Will advocated by Schopenhauer

(the philosopher is specifically cited by Schoenberg on the previous page), we are invited to see the goal of ever more aspiring self-expression as its own annihilation. Only when sorrow at the failure of the Will to fabricate a revelation has given way to resignation might the true revelation be granted, whose divine content is of its nature to be conceived as cool and icy, and beyond "animal warmth".

If this is the moment when we come closest to the actual expressive world of Gustav Mahler (in the symphony he nevertheless regarded as his most tragic!), so also is it the point where obtuseness alone could prevent us from seeing this essay as a most valuable document in the case-study of Schoenberg's own creative quest for an art of mystical revelation from which all elements of conventional subjectivity have systematically and artificially been eliminated. This would be achieved by an organizational principle that would ensure that the totality of the work would be derived from its initial inspiration:

> The inspiration is not the theme, but the whole work. And it is not the one who writes a good theme who is inventive, but the one to whom a whole symphony occurs at once.[25]
>
> ... it is entirely out of the question for someone to accomplish something masterly in any respect who is not a master in every respect.[26]

Ever more surely are we led to an understanding that the increasing concern for organization in Schoenberg's own creative work defined an aim for self-expression that was in reality a *flight* both from expression itself and from the lesser mortals who would seek to possess by 'understanding'. Speaking of Mahler's struggle for clarity and perfection, Schoenberg even observes that "... music assures the divine prerogative of anonymity of feelings, of obscurity for the uninitiated...."[27]

Note that it is a *divine* prerogative! Are we not returned to the image of the burning apostle who bears within himself the "image of a god" solely by virtue of the "halo of sanctity" that marks him out? Self-expression for the truly great artist is almost one with the medieval notion of divine *imitatio* – the universal Word of God within him is to be revealed only by ascetic suppression of his own subjective particularity: "... there is only one content, which all great men wish to express: the longing of mankind for its future form, for an immortal soul, for dissolution into the universe – the longing of the soul for its God."[28] And if Schoenberg still judiciously speaks only of "longing" here (are we to see Mahler longing for what Schoenberg himself was to achieve?), his subsequent mystical definition of genius is clear enough:

> Talent grows by acquiring capacities which already existed outside of itself; it assimilates these, and finally even possesses them. Genius already possesses all its future faculties from the very beginning. It only develops them; it merely unwinds, unrolls, unfolds them.[29]

As the essay draws towards its conclusion, Schoenberg again suggests that Mahler only gradually and latterly approached the high artistic goal of divine revelation through human asceticism. Echoing his earlier assessment of the expressive achievement of the

Sixth Symphony, he has the following to say of the Ninth:

> This symphony is no longer couched in the personal tone. It consists, so to speak, of objective, almost passionless statements of a beauty which becomes perceptible only to one who can dispense with animal warmth and feels at home in spiritual coolness.[30]

Mahler's failure to complete the Tenth Symphony is inevitably, as we now see, to be described as a failure to solve "the riddles of this world". The solution is thus relegated to a future to which the artistic genius lights the way that we must strive to follow in search of the "higher reality" and "our immortal soul":[31] "We are to remain blind until we have acquired eyes. Eyes that see the future. Eyes that penetrate more than the sensual, which is only a likeness; that penetrate the supersensual."[32]

*   *   *

Beyond the quirky mannerisms of Schoenberg's written style – the oddly overwrought visionary tone, the frequently threatened self-revelation as Messiah – a startlingly clear exposition of his most secret philosophy of art is to be found in this essay. Behind the image of Mahler is to be seen a more complete likeness of Schoenberg than may be found in any photograph or almost any biographical or critical study of him. He is not Adrian Leverkühn, nor is he quite the Progressive Artist of Adorno's *Philosophy* – though his concern with non-subjectively determined expressive truth is thoroughly in accord with Adorno's analysis. The tragedy detailed both by the novelist and the philosopher nevertheless finds a potent exemplar in the father of musical modernism, whose quest for expressive truth proves latterly to have turned wholly into a quest for the revelatory word of a tortuously conceived God. Rather than being manifest in his creation, this God was considered logically definable only in terms of all that his creation was not. Shamefaced and disillusioned in all his doings, the Progressive Artist becomes ascetic renunciant, for all that he might hide his agony behind the daemonic mask of the seer-Faust that was his birthright.

In view of the role that Schoenberg has played in twentieth-century music, it must be considered a mercy that Adorno was able to discern cultural and social necessity in what might otherwise have proved but a bizarrely fanatical excursion down one of the many dead-end roads of *fin-de-siècle* mysticism. One nevertheless wonders quite how many of those who followed Schoenberg into his particular Arctic wasteland had thought of looking at the sketches for the 'necessarily unfinished' revelation of Mahler's Tenth Symphony. Schoenberg's essay might well have granted them insight into certain of the anguished tensions and expressive dichotomies upon which it turns. They might also have registered the dire portent of the muffled drum-strokes with which its Finale opens – and observed that when it ends it really doesn't sound a bit like Schoenberg.

SIX

Chaos, the Machine or the Mystic Word

I

> I cannot warn often enough against the over-
> valuation of these analyses, since they lead only to
> what I have always fought against – the recog-
> nition of how the piece is *made*; whereas I have
> always helped my students to recognize – what it
> is! I have tried to make that comprehensible to
> Wiesengrund [– Adorno] and also to Berg and
> Webern. But they do not believe me.
>
> Schoenberg in a letter to Kolisch of July 1932[1]

The difficulty of getting people to attend to the aesthetic results rather than the constructional principles
of his art was a matter to which Schoenberg returned
in exasperation on more than one occasion. Yet if he
was unable to persuade Berg, Webern and Adorno
together, we might be forgiven for suggesting that the
chances of his persuading anyone else were slim indeed. The problem was that he himself gave little

indication as to what form such aesthetic evaluation might take. Where the errant Adorno was so brilliantly to indicate how the adverse, 'commonsense' response of critics and audiences to the shocks of the Master's music might in fact be incorporated into a positively charged comprehension of its philosophical basis, Schoenberg himself habitually either denied the shocking strangeness of his music ("I am convinced that, one day, it will be recognized how closely this 'something new' is related to the best models of the past . . ."[2]) or rewarded the curious lay enquirer with elucidations that lead directly back to technical and analytic considerations that serve only to heighten the mystification. Such an enquirer into the Variations for Orchestra, op. 31, will derive enigmatic enlightenment indeed from Schoenberg's comments to Erwin Stein on the work,[3] or his statement in *Style and Idea*: "I used in many places a device, derived from double counterpoint of the tenth and twelfth, which allows the addition of parallel thirds to every part involved."[4]

Our enquirer might well be led by such statements to suspect that Schoenberg's ideas, like his later musical style, could be of interest only to other twentieth-century composers of the most advanced and 'difficult' variety, who needed to adopt remarkable stratagems whereby to allow themselves to write in parallel thirds. Would he be entirely wrong in imagining that in the everyday world such stratagems were of more relevance to the inmates of mental institutions than the average concert-goer? No doubt there were experts who understood these things and the constructional problems that suddenly seemed to have grown in importance, to the total exclusion of content, of expression or communication.

The question I pose here, with historical hindsight that takes account of the manifest potency of the Schoenberg phenomenon, is this: Can we now reassure that bewildered enquirer that, after all, Schoenberg's style and ideas, and the problems that stemmed from them, were as natural to him as they have proved consequently necessary to other 'advanced' composers? Can we, in short, respond to Schoenberg's own request for a critical evaluation of his works that goes beyond their organizational idiosyncracies; can we redeem him for humanity at large in a way converse to that in which the all-too-human Tchaikovsky has in recent years been redeemed for post-Schoenbergian analysts by the discovery that his music is, after all, rigorously organized?

The end-product of such a process of critical redemption might be a deepened understanding of the curious gulf that appeared to exist between Schoenberg's writings about his own music and the way in which he wanted people to respond to it (we recall his longing "to be taken for a better sort of Tchaikovsky"[5]). Having bridged that gulf we might be led further to understand Schoenberg's crucial, if ambivalent position as father-figure of 'modern music' in the West, not in fact with respect to matters of musical technique and language so much as the extraordinary intellectual relationship that came to exist between him and his chosen art-form.

★ ★ ★

It may be that the ultimate limitation of Adorno's brilliant assessment of Schoenberg in his *Philosophy of Modern Music* lies in the extent to which he allows his own philosophical preoccupations to inform his demonstration of how the twentieth century *might* value Schoenberg without sufficiently considering such evidence as does exist as to whether Schoenberg himself would have seen it that way. The initial point of divergence may be located in a not uncharacteristic absorption in metaphorical comparison between the processes of Schoenberg's early 'free atonal' works and those of the Freudian unconscious: by registering undisguised the emotions of the unconscious, these works were to be considered "case studies in the sense of psychoanalytic dream case studies."[6]

Adorno allowed himself to make a curious error here (which he only inadvertently put right when discussing Schoenberg's later music[7]). We may accept that Schoenberg's rigorous self-denial of the unauthenticated cliché was a function of his growing belief, in the first decade of this century, that the tonal language of his contemporaries and immediate forebears was at best unwittingly prey to 'untruth'. To suggest that his own works of the period attained an immediate truthfulness of expression by virtue of registering direct outbursts of energy from the unconscious is probably to misunderstand the very nature of art, and certainly to give a false impression of the nature of music. For while Kandinsky could indeed stand, paint-pots to hand, and attack a canvas in a momentary outburst of expressionistic anguish, no such momentary spasm in the presence of manuscript paper could produce scores such as those of the Five Orchestral Pieces or *Erwartung* (rapid though the composition of the latter may have been). The precise musical equivalent of a Kandinsky 'Improvisation' would be the tape of an extempore performance. Whatever the nature of the musical language, large-scale orchestral scores must be planned and executed with great care if they are to achieve the effect of a spontaneous outburst. In fact, in accordance with Adorno's general notion of the 'philosophy' of art, Schoenberg's early expressionist works are the reverse of case-studies – or at least of material that could be *used* in a case-study simply as it stands. For that one would have to turn to the works of Schoenberg's tonal forebears who, suffering from the perhaps deluded belief that they *were* 'expressing' emotions, were thus permitted unguardedly to reveal themselves to those whose business was the scrutiny of emotional indulgence (or synthesis, or whatever we decide is really happening). Schoenberg's awareness of the problems led him to create music which was purely a graphic model of the new picture of the mind that had in fact been outlined in Freud's *Traumdeutung* of 1901. It is as if only one way appeared open to Schoenberg by which to avoid the puppet-horror of appearing to engage in a wilful dance that was really only a symptomatic response to the primitive functioning of the chaotic unconscious. His music would become the frozen illustration of a terrifying idea. The notoriously 'unanalysable' *Erwartung* represents no spontaneous eruption from unconscious depths, but rather marks a final stage in the stormy nineteenth-century romance between music and ideas. Where knowledge, in Nietzsche's interpretation of *Hamlet*,[8] inhibited action, so ideas finally press music into total submission. Schoenberg's music becomes the mirror of an intellectual proposition that must inspire despair: all that we thought we did in the name of expression and will was but the outward manifestation of an inner chaos. This chaos might be said to reveal Nature in her truest, early twentieth-century aspect as the reverse of what she had appeared to the eighteenth-century mind. Schoenberg's famous monodrama, with its unashamedly 'Freudian' text by Marie Pappenheim, is thus a musical model – rigorously intended in its every surprise, its every avoidance of the conventional mannerisms of musical extension and textual accompaniment – of a mind that has lost its soul, has lost the beloved who reflects a consolatory image of the willing ego. What we searched for was never there at all. There were only the blind forces that prompted the search. The realization brings in its wake as clear a state of alienation and despairing disillusionment as one can find in twentieth-century art. The final lines of the Woman's monologue, lost in the forests of the unconscious, run as follows:

> Oh I cursed you . . .
> but your compassion made me happy . . .
> I believed, was happy . . .
> *(Stillness. Dawn in the East beneath*
> *distant clouds through which a faint*
> *light shines – a yellowish gleam like*
> *candlelight.)*

Dearest, dearest, morning is coming . . .
What do I do here alone? . . .
In this never-ending life . . .
In this formless, colourless dream . . .
For my world was defined by your presence and
    all the colours of the world were shed
    from your eyes . . .
The light comes for all . . . but
I, alone, in my night?
The morning parts us . . . always the morning . . .
So dark is your parting kiss . . .
Once more an endless day of waiting . . .
Oh, indeed you wake no more.
People in their thousands pass by . . .
I no longer recognize you.
All alive, their eyes ablaze . . .
Where are you?
It is dark . . . your kiss a flaming sign in my night.
My lips burn and shine . . . towards you . . .
Oh you are there . . .
I was searching . . .[9]

★   ★   ★

There is every reason why serious students of twentieth-century music should have tended to regard the
years 1908–9 as those in which Schoenberg produced
the first consummate works of his maturity (the
Second String Quartet, the *George Lieder*, op. 15, the
op. 11 Piano Pieces and *Erwartung*). There is no
question that the earlier, tonal works have gained

much in the reflected light of Schoenberg's later career and have been somewhat over-valued. Yet how dark a step was it that Schoenberg had to take in order to find himself – a step that entailed doubting that there was any self to find. The tattered remnants of subjective expression are to be discerned only in the partly psychotic demonstration of his lonely mission as artist-explorer and artist-martyr that is embarrassingly explicit in the appalling text of *Die glückliche Hand* but which more subtly and movingly underpins the programmatic structure of the Second String Quartet. Beyond this the music is increasingly subsumed by the extra-musical idea that truth can now only be expressed negatively; in fact by the ascetic avoidance of all expressive indulgence. The Romantic belief that awareness itself sunders us from Nature and keeps us from heaven now finds its ironic confirmation in an art that, as a kind of penance for the horrifying acceptance of inner chaos and emptiness as the transcendent truth of modern self-awareness, is condemned to invoke that chaos with all the organizational rigour that Wagner had once used to synthesize his dramas of redemption, or Mahler to 'answer' the questions of life and celebrate the will.

Of course part of it was just modish expressionistic nonsense, and Schoenberg was never at his best when trying to keep up with the times. Franz Marc's wife saw to the heart of it all after a 1912 pilgrimage to hear *Pierrot Lunaire* in Munich:

> We were rather disappointed: the whole affair is too strongly Viennese – Egon Schiele, Klimt, – also like Schoenberg's heads with green eyes. We

were naturally interested and a lot of it was certainly good. But the whole thing is not really pure. The element of sentimentality which the piece contains takes away one's confidence, even if one likes a lot of it. I prefer the futurists.[10]

At its most musically productive in the vaguely spiritualistic intimations of the second of the op. 11 Piano Pieces, at its worst in the *Glückliche Hand* text and the ghoulish painted 'visions' referred to by Frau Marc, the expressionist manner tended consistently towards violent catastrophe on the one hand (achieved in the third of the op. 11 Piano Pieces and the first and fourth of the Five Orchestral Pieces) and, on the other, the ultimately more important encephalographic models of involuntary subterranean mental life that are so brilliantly achieved in *Erwartung* and the last of the Five Orchestral Pieces (the 'Obbligato Recitative').

I describe these as more important not only for the reason that they most comprehensively foreshadow the manner of Schoenberg's later works, but that they already embody a response to a yet more disturbing proposition about the now defunct 'expressing subject' than that his fabricated order was but the outward aspect of chaotic promptings. In the strangely internalized anti-metaphysics of the twentieth century, the model of spiritual emptiness and fruitlessness that had been based upon the concept of natural chaos was to be replaced by one based upon a despairingly inverted interpretation of man's own most 'useful' creation – the machine. While the whirring, whirling and clanking monsters of nineteenth-century industrialism were to be equated explicitly with social repression and regimentation by Fritz Lang in *Metropolis* and Chaplin in *Modern Times,* Schoenberg, as post-Wagnerian German Artist on an *inward* journey of discovery, most subtly and horrifically discovered their potency as images of a mental life from which the soul had fled. From a musical metaphor of mental activity as an unwilled series of volcanic eruptions from the unconscious, we move to one where even the (however involuntary) *form* of the explosion is renounced for the timeless ticking of inner clocks, the whispering of fly-wheels and the flickering of electronic needles upon unwatched dials. Already in the first serial works (whose rhythmic regularity has mistakenly been re-garded as a mere function of the regressive neo-classicism evinced in titles like 'Suite' and 'Variations') Schoenberg was producing graphic musi-cal cartoons of a literally self-denying view of mental life. Only the behaviourists would seek to interpret such a view in a positive light, seeing the driverless machine as one that could at least be influenced by external reinforcement or the opposite (the out-of-control vehicle could not be stopped, but by building walls you might direct it out of harm's way).

There are manifest signs in Schoenberg's greatest serial works, however, that the image was indeed still a *repressive* one for him. It is precisely here that we might return to the op. 31 Variations for Orchestra, to whose human and aesthetic content Schoenberg him-self provided so little access in his comments about "double counterpoint of the tenth . . .". And of course it is once more precisely an *anti*-human content for the most part. Far from being a gesture of relative human warmth (as it has often been described), the diminished seventh to which the parts comply in the opening bars serves only to heighten the clarity of an image of the first tickings and revolutions within a complex piece of musical machinery that is, as it were, being started up. The theme, when it comes at bar 34, is at once a function of the metrical impulse characteristic of the neo-classical aspect of Schoenberg's serial style and a threnody, by virtue of the crystallized elements of the Mahlerian song that it contains – elements that had nevertheless been still, if agonizingly, alive in the expressionistic outburst of bars 19 to 23, as they will constantly re-emerge in similar, potentially disruptive fashion throughout the Variations. Whereas the theme itself represents a model of nihilistic repose, it is not uninteresting that when the expressionistic blood courses, it repeatedly does so in the manner of the high, tortured screams of the string writing of the late Mahler as he wrestled in the throes of extreme existential crisis (and it is vital to observe that Schoenberg here looks back to Mahler as much as ever Mahler 'looked forward' to Schoenberg). The immediate response to this outburst in the Introduction is fascinating: *wieder ruhig*, the machine is brought back under control with a mysterious trombone enunciation of the B–A–C–H motive which will recur recognizably throughout the work as a kind of mystical invocation. For Bach, after all, the relentless and however painful working out of strict counterpoint, which in Schoenberg takes on the aspect of a meaninglessly intricate mechanism without transcendent purpose, was an image of *God's* purpose which would always reach final resolution in the eternal peace of the unambiguous cadence.

Could it be that the relentless, however undirected *order* of the machine-music – and the work is cast in the form of die-stamped variations – represents both an image of repression and the outcome of an act of ordering without which the disruptive screams of existential awareness would simply rend us and the work apart (as indeed they had once done in Schoenberg's expressionist phase)? What makes the Variations so fascinating and even moving is the extent to which the elements of the dialectic remain for once *active* in almost literally Mahlerian fashion. While the 'Waltz' of Variation IV successfully submerges the singing theme in the noise of the metrical machinery, Variation V is once again all expressionistic screaming before the 'voice' is then whittled down in preparation for the renewed metrical order of Variation VI. What, then, could be the role of the B–A–C–H motive in this work? Might its role as prayerful invocation look to a transcendent purpose *from outside* (what had been God's Law to Bach) to redeem the horror of the complimentary images of mental life otherwise proposed here: those of disruptive chaos on the one hand and the repressive futility of the machine on the other?

★ ★ ★

We might readily interpret the B–A–C–H motive of the op. 31 Variations as the symbolic, outward emblem of the mystic word that permeates the whole composition as the basic set or twelve-tone row from which its textures are derived. To do so without further comment would nevertheless be to overlook the role of self-abnegation in Schoenberg's last-ditch, tragically intellectualized version of the "Erbarmen!" of Mahler's Tenth Symphony. Instead of the agonized reacceptance of the self, leading to the transfigured simplicity of the flute solo, that is undergone in the Finale of that work, Schoenberg effects something much more in accord with his belief that that same (to him 'unfinished') Finale might rather contain intimations of a mystic truth *beyond* the self.[11]

Although the Variations conclude nihilistically in a sell-out to conventional form (a *presto* coda à la Bartók finally bursts in for the kill at bar 508), the subtlety of the underlying organizational principle considered as a mystical *act,* and thus the reverse of any imagined *statement* of actual revelation, is highlighted by Roberto Gerhard in the beautiful sleeve-notes that he wrote for the CBS recording under Robert Craft.[12] Their beauty lies precisely in the fact that, starting with an explicit reference to Schoenberg's concern about serial analysis, they allow of precisely that kind of descriptive *aperçu* that illuminates and invites sympathy where Schoenberg's own explanations tend to alienate and mystify. Yet the nature of the comparisons made by Gerhard, as a true Schoenbergian, are revealing indeed. His description of the first Variation provides a felicitous version of the image that I have myself used of an internal landscape of unwilled electrical activity: "The eventuation spreads over the entire auditory field, which takes the aspect of a vast mosaic made up of short, nervous motives flashing by like Morse signals, partly overlapping. This is an exciting, beautifully 'aerated' texture. . . ." What is important is that he invites us to find beauty rather than horror in the flickering procession of these undecipherable Morse signals. Fascinatingly, Gerhard has little to say of the passages of expressionistic *Angst,* while more fascinating still is the botanical, or more often *bio-chemical* nature of the admiring similes elsewhere employed: "As used by Schoenberg in op. 31, serial order affects internal organization only. It is a molecular order which – unlike the DNA molecule – carries but a limited amount of *genetic* information." His description of Variation V is particularly rich in this respect:

> Variation V increases the distancing process, the traits of the progenitor being hardly discernible in the offspring. Kinship is no longer overtly manifest; it has to be looked for in the 'constitution' – only the blood-group reveals it, so to speak. . . . How this distantiation is effected without relaxation or severing of links with the basic row is of interest to the analyst alone; suffice it to mention here that the 'constitution' shows the tone-row fibres no longer spreading horizontally, but vertically folding and twisting upon themselves, as tightly bundled together as chromosome packages.

It is no wonder that the interest of the 'analyst' suddenly resurfaces here, or that Gerhard had in his initial admonitions (". . . listening to music is not an analytical process") been led to observe: "Yet, inversely, there is no substitute for analysis, for slow, painstaking analysis, as often as not quite as taxing as cipher-decoding, if what is wanted is knowledge of serial organization . . .". For what Gerhard is celebrating in these notes is precisely a kind of music wherein the nineteenth-century German artist's desire for redemption (*Erlösung dem Erlöser* indeed!), while emasculated by a total collapse of belief in the self as a basis for the expression of transcendent truth, has guiltily adopted the objective observational zeal of the natural-scientist as the only permissible basis for affective enthusiasm. It is a music which seeks not *imitatio Dei* but *imitatio naturae*; that the work should become a model of scientifically perceived nature rather than a troubling mirror of the self. And how readily may we see this goal in Schoenberg's case fitting in with that image of art as a spiritual exercise in self-abnegation. The composer himself had, in his essay on Mahler, described the aim of this exercise as the generation of "cool, icy comfort . . . bestowed from a height which is reached only by one who soars to resignation"; "only he can hear it who understands what heavenly voices whisper without animal warmth."[13]

Only in the crystalline, microscopic truths of nature herself, in a realm where man's devalued will must be abandoned in favour of patient, prayerfully expectant yet humble attention, may the mystic word be sought – be it in the double helix of DNA or the still unfathomable configuration of quarks within the atom. Could it be that by compelling the hitherto subjectively determined rules of musical language to comply with just such an arbitrary 'law' as may be found in nature (the serial principle) and just as necessary an admixture of accidental chaos as is found in nature (here the subjective whim that may determine rhythmic patterns and textural density) we might accidentally hit upon, or release, the Word of God? Had not all other attempts to picture God provided only images of ourselves? Was not Schoenberg in this respect still most ardently seeking an art from which the material for no case-study of *himself* might be extracted? And does not *Moses und Aron* turn ultimately upon the recognition that, whether in the unintentional revelations of subjective expression or the equally unintentional revelations of a rigorously adopted aesthetic discipline of self-abnegation, the however carefully fashioned window always turns into a mirror?

In this culminatory masterpiece, not only is any mystical, emblematic representation of the Row comparable to the B–A–C–H motive in the Variations avoided; one might say that the absolute *necessity* of such avoidance lies at the heart of the work's tragic import as epitaph to the Romantic Artist within Schoenberg himself. For the work, in its so eloquently *un*finished form, is the opposite of a mystical revelation, though the tragedy derives precisely from the absolute acceptance of both the possibility and necessity *of* such a revelation (which is clearly and unequivocally suffered by Moses just prior to the raising of the curtain upon Scene 1 and while absent in Act II). On this intellectual cross is Schoenberg crucified both as aspiring seer and artist with a place in society. Here the Romantic artist-as-outsider finds his last, bitterly self-tortured image. Without the expressively naive artist-Aron who 'gives the people what they want', the riven and intellectually ascetic artist-Moses (whose one moment of song in an otherwise *spoken* role accompanies his plea to Aron: "purify your thinking!") would have no goal to which to aspire as Aron's truth-seeking converse. Moses needs Aron, but is the reverse true? Not surprisingly, it is Aron's imagined "land where milk and honey flow" that finally mobilizes the Israelites at the end of Act I, rather than Moses' highly dubious promise: "In the wasteland pureness of thought will provide you nurture, sustain and advance you."[14]

In denying the however flawed truth of his own humanity, Moses – like the Schoenberg who devised a system whereby to destroy his own musical language for whatever apparently impeccable reasons – sets himself firmly upon the path that will lead him to the point where he will in desperation destroy the tablets bearing the Word with which he *had* been entrusted. The tragic climax of the work had previously come in the catastrophic self-indictment: "My love is for my idea, I live just for it!".[15] The final double irony of his last admission of defeat – "O Word! – thou Word that I lack!"[16] – is painfully registered both in the fact that it gives quite literally upon silence (for the textually vastly inferior Third Act was never, of course, set) and that it is uttered just as the Music, in that long solo string line that harks back to the initiating viola recitative of Mahler's Tenth Symphony, seemed set to begin again; as if, indeed, at last in unwilled response to the agonized invocation of half a lifetime.

II

We are now in a position where we may see Schoenberg as a terminal figure of Stygian authority in the
context of the German tradition to which he so consistently asserted his allegiance. So too may we see why
his most influential pupils should have doggedly
shadowed the intimately ordained necessity of his
avoidance of any direct critical engagement with the
disturbed and disturbing *content* of his works, at the
expense of a technologically optimistic preoccupation
with stylistic and organizational matters (for all that
Schoenberg might himself have come to warn against
such a preoccupation). If Schoenberg's hitherto
unassailable position in the histories of twentieth-
century music as father of technical innovation and
stylistic 'progress' must suffer ironic inversion when
considered in this light, his myriad would-be succes-
sors and torch-bearers inevitably take on the aspect
of epiphenomena, of limpets and barnacles desperately
clinging to a sinking ship.

That Schoenberg was indeed, in however macabre a
fashion, 'father' of the whole avant-garde movement in
twentieth-century Western music can be demonstrated
precisely in the extent to which the music of its
protagonists was to remain in thrall as the graphic
shadow of ideas, the demonstrative prey of intellectual
propositions. None of the footnote-writers to Schoenberg's ambivalent achievement have, for example, as-
sisted so blithely and comprehensively in the posthumous operation of the Master's self-imposed curse

as John Cage, who was even, appropriately enough, a pupil of the ageing composer at the University of California, Los Angeles, in the 1940s. Cage rejected the machine, seeing in it an image of the repressive capitalist technology of the culture he sought to renew. Nevertheless, as one of the first of the Californian 'flower people' (expert on mushrooms and whimsically childlike devotee of Zen Buddhism), he logically joined the other two poles of Schoenberg's triune cosmology, to bring about an expressive absence more wilfully total than was ever to be found in Schoenberg. For Cage, Nature, arbitrarily conceived *as* Chaos, unequivocally provides the Mystic Word. And where Schoenberg sought desperately to exclude deluding human warmth by adopting a technical process that ensured the decimation of conventional expressive vocabulary and gesture, Cage, rather in the spirit of Gerhard's eagerly scientific response to the resulting simulacra of natural forms, blithely substitutes for all residual acts of creative choice the invocation of Chaos in ritualized chance operations. The dice are thrown, the pebbles tossed on to the music-paper and their locations marked. Cage logically equates the process with the operation of the Chinese *I Ching*. Yet where folk-seers versed in tea-leaves or the splayed entrails of sacrificial lambs might indeed divine wisdom from such accidentally created ciphers, Cage, rejoicing in a technique that "fails to control the elements subjected to it",[17] produces 'works' that are to be taken at their lightest as whimsical admonitions (reminding us that we really should find life more interesting than art), at their most philosophically portentous as celebrations of the very truth of which Schoenberg could not allow himself to admit: that redeeming, transcendent truth itself, far from being 'inexpressible', simply did not exist. "Well, the grand thing about the human mind", says Cage, "is that it can turn its own tables and see meaninglessness as ultimate meaning."[18] ". . . Here we are. Let us say Yes to our presence together in Chaos."[19]

But in attitude and word, not music. Cage has given up even the attempt to find the music for the New Man that might correspond to his many words about him (that remain charmingly, subversively coherent *as* words for all the formal conceits whereby he affects to turn them back into music and obscure their rationality). While Cage may act the Fool to Schoenberg's tormented Faust, there is no question but that they play out their roles in the same tragedy. Around and between them are grouped the leading *dramatis personae* of the avant-garde, all self-condemned in various ways and in varying degrees to follow their master on his ill-fated course between purposeless Chaos and the equally purposeless, repressive Machine, in search of the Mystic Word that might restore to us the courage to fight off the so very modern fears that would engulf us. Even those covetors of the white coat of the passive, data-collecting scientist who are happy to substitute simulacra of nature for the mystic word (swapping mandala for maze) are condemned still to produce models of chaos that may yet be articulated with the unfathomable regimen of unthinkable machines – and it is no accident that would-be composers show signs of becoming outnumbered by eager 'analysts' in the corridors of musical academia.

The post-Schoenbergian protagonists of the avant-garde (how ironic the term becomes!) to whom I have referred, whatever the nature of their fears or the complexion and cast of their imagined answers and mystic intimations, all share with Schoenberg an art that has been subsumed by ideas, be they crass or profound. Criticism of their music therefore can only and must be criticism of their ideas, which are not surprisingly to be found more and more in published form: in introductions and appendices to works, in tracts and treatises or books of conversations. (Might we put it that the programme music of the nineteenth century has simply given way to the music programme in our own?) And to how startling a degree do these philosophical pamphlets take on the aspect of footnotes to Schoenberg, half a century after his first serial works!

Here, for example, is Stockhausen (1971) enlarging upon one of the ideas by which his compositions were for a time dominated. In this the Mystic Word is unequivocally sought in the 'matrices' of natural forms:

> The fantastic concept of the matrix is that in every atom there's a complete world. The more complex the species, the less ability there is to reproduce the limbs and parts of the body. But potentially every cell of the body contains the complete matrix of the whole body – of you not of someone else.... That's what happens in *Mantra*. The mantra of *Mantra* is a thirteen-note formula which is blown up to sixty-three minutes. It's always this mantra, whose largest

proportions just represent the same proportions of the initial mantra. It's one seed which brings about an enormous tree, a whole world.[20]

At about the same time (between 1972 and 1974), Pierre Boulez was engaged in a series of interviews with Célestin Deliège, which were published in 1975. As well as registering a number of fascinating and at times critical insights into the whole post-Schoen-bergian modernist enterprise, Boulez himself reveals much about his own earlier and more orthodox avant-garde preoccupations. It is in the chapter entitled 'Expansion of serial techniques' that he speaks of his concern in the 1950s "to see how it might be possible to reconstitute a way of writing that begins with something which eliminates personal invention."[21] He goes on to describe what he himself now sees as the element of wilful "absurdity" (foreshadowing the beginning of a personal victory over post-Schoen-bergian 'complexes' about organization) present in *Structures*, the first piece of which (1951) was based on material borrowed from Messiaen's *Mode de valeurs et d'intensités*:

> ... thus I had material that I had not invented and for whose invention I deliberately rejected all responsibility in order to see just how far it was possible to go.... this sort of absurdity, of chaos and mechanical wheels-within-wheels tending al-most towards the random, was completely inten-tional and has probably been one of my most fundamental experiments as a composer.[22]

As if, one might add, there were anything peculiar to Boulez about such an experiment!

For a final example I turn to the leading representative of a more recent generation, whose works, and
whose commentaries upon them, show every sign of
synthesizing a final *ne plus ultra* of orthodox avant-
garde conservatism. The aural effect of Brian
Ferneyhough's *Time and Motion Study II* "for singing cellist and live electronics" (1973–6) is, alas, that
of a vestigial remnant of experimental student-
improvisation from the 1960s. The composer's expla-
natory note, however, represents a most fascinating
late manifestation of that curse upon Western musical
expression whose greatest and sole legitimate victim
was Schoenberg himself. From Ferneyhough's
remarkable concatenation of scientific and philosophical intimations, I quote the following:

> The second half of *Time and Motion Study II* ...
> witnesses the rapid climb to predominance of the
> tendency towards entropy inherent in the method
> of electronic intervention employed. In his
> desperation in the face of the sudden increase in
> the amount of superfluous "memory fragments"
> hemming him aurally in, the cellist commences a
> "dialogue" with the apparatus and the sounds
> which torture and frustrate him. The text (reduced
> to a string of key words) deals with the impos-
> sibility of attaining a harmony between words
> and emotional states.... The cellist plays without
> electronic commentary at only one moment, and
> that right at the end. Having at last achieved a
> degree of independence, the cellist finds himself
> reduced to endlessly repeating slight variations of
> the same meaningless tone. The absurdity of the
> situation is underlined by the fact that the perfor-
> mer is condemned to continue to the bitter end in

the certain knowledge that all recorded tapes – his "memory" – are being steadily erased behind his back.[23]

"O Wort, du Wort ... das mir fehlt!" Time takes on the aspect of a relentless machine that ceaselessly moves the individual on beyond the moments of awareness from which he might construct his song – whose elements are thus reduced to the chaotic circling of "slight variations of the same meaningless tone". Sad indeed the brave new world that has such cellists in it.

* * *

My assertion, then, must be that a broadly critical consideration of Schoenberg's achievement may lead indeed to his redemption for humanity as a figure of profound and seminal pathos, beyond the local manifestations of paranoia and self-lacerating intellectual fanaticism. The paradox must be that such a critical reassessment of its nature entails a drastic revision of his long-established position as innovator and progressive. Such 'innovation' and 'progress' in musical language and compositional procedure must also be considered under the aspect of their extraordinary conceptual determinants. In this Schoenberg can only be regarded as a terminal phenomenon, a further consequence of which must be the need for an equally comprehensive critical reassessment of the subsequent modernist movement in music, whose every eager experiment, every philosophical proposition and mannerism may so readily be seen to be subsumed in the tragically failed quest of Schoenberg's own intellectual and creative life. Yet if criticism of the modernist phenomenon must consequently focus primarily upon the ideas to which Western 'classical' music has all but been sacrificed, a still more important critical task is suggested: namely that of assessing the alternative tradition of those who, by retaining some subjective contact with the traditional expressive means of music, have brought down upon themselves the accusation of being cultural regressives, irrelevant neo-romantics, *conservatives,* in the highly successful propaganda campaign of the avant-garde. The initial task must be to establish the criteria of a kind of progress that has nothing necessarily to do with linguistic or constructional innovation, but is registered initially within precisely that realm of ideas and values whose atrophy we have traced in the conceits of the orthodox modernists. Being largely posthumous, the task can in no wise be taken as easy, and ever before us must be the recognition that these same modernists may now claim the horror of two World Wars and the knowledge of Auschwitz to support their assertion that no harmony of style and idea with subjective expressive intention in music can have any valid basis beyond that of evasion and self-indulgent nostalgia.

SEVEN

Palestrina and the
Dangerous Futurists

A previously almost taboo question that has been
raised by recent talk of a 'tonal backlash' in new music
is whether a vital and contemporary work can be conceived without a correspondingly progressive stylistic language. If the readoption by composers of types
of consonance and even chordal progressions associated with traditional tonality signifies a facile or evasive yearning for past comforts, then the question
would appear to be answered. For who, in this brave
new world of art made necessarily ascetic by the
horrifying clichés of popular culture in a mass society,
would wish to associate music with mere hedonism?
Furthermore, the very idea that some mysterious 'content' can be isolated from language would be regarded
as heretical in the extreme by many modern theorists.

Something of this same awkward question was in
fact publicly aired as long ago as 1917. It was raised by
the composer of an opera, first performed in that year,
whose very subject-matter reflected deep concern
about the implications of what we might retro-

spectively consider orthodox modernist ideas about progress and change in twentieth-century European music – ideas that were then, of course, only just beginning to be formed. The ideas to which I refer depended, as we have seen, upon a self-conscious relationship between the composer and his musical language, and relied upon an iconoclastic mistrust of popular concepts and traditional mannerisms of expression.

I have suggested that Schoenberg's flight from conventional expression through the carefully fabricated hysteria and inner chaos of expressionism to the mystic abnegation of serialism could on one level be seen as a profoundly German symptom of precisely that *fin-de-siècle* decadence that in Russia produced the pre-Cagean antics of Obukhov and Skryabin's engagingly crazy project for a world-dissolving Mysterium of philosophically charged musical eroticism. In the realm of purely critical thought, we have found such a view best countered by the equally serious and Germanically rigorous advocacy of Theodor Adorno. Far surpassing the propagandists and musico-theoretical enthusiasts, Adorno, in his *Philosophy of Modern Music,* was to indicate with impressive force the particular expressive and social 'truth' of Schoenberg's apparently anti-expressive and anti-social music. From the traumatic shocks of the earliest atonal works to the frozen labyrinths of the mature serial compositions, Adorno traced a quest after 'progressive truth' that necessarily sought to escape from the bourgeois audience that supported modern mass society with its pressures of mass-production; pressures that heralded a new kind of barbarism, antipathetic to the freedom and integrity of the individual spirit. Tragically, Adorno observed, Schoenberg's bid for freedom led him to impose upon himself a new kind of enchaining coercion; but perhaps it could not be otherwise. Adorno ultimately considered Schoenberg's art to be fully vindicated in its aspect as the openly revealed symptom of a sickness that the world might otherwise have sought to deny.

★   ★   ★

In June 1925, Thomas Mann penned an interesting reply to a rather curious letter of fiftieth-birthday congratulations that he had received from the patriotic German composer Hans Pfitzner. Pfitzner's opera *Palestrina* had so impressed Mann on its first perform-ance in 1917 that he had included an essay on it in his *Betrachtungen eines Unpolitischen,* completed in 1918.[1] This admiring essay, however, while decrying the sterile philistinism of democratic 'virtue', already evinced ambivalent feelings about incipient German decadence and "sympathy with death" that were to bear fruit in *The Magic Mountain* and his ostensibly anti-German political convictions of the 1920s. It was Mann's subsequent expression of these convictions that led Pfitzner to temper his birthday congratula-tions with the recognition of "a confrontation between us".[2] Mann's courteous reply alluded to the hero (Hans Castorp) of *The Magic Mountain,* whom he had described there as "life's delicate child":

> All of us artists are delicate children of life, but children of life none the less, and – this now pertains to the musician with his romantic licence as well as the literary artist – whoever, at a moment such as this in Europe, does not take sides with the party of life and the future against fascination with death, would truly be an idle boy....[3]

It is interesting that in his final analysis of the specifically German malaise that he saw at the heart of modern Europe's problems Mann should, in *Doctor Faustus*, have relied heavily upon Adorno's critique of Schoenberg when creating his "tragic hero", the composer Adrian Leverkühn. It was of course highly relevant to Mann's purpose to indicate that the most complex trappings of progressive musical modernism masked a variety of that same German disease that he had, however fondly, diagnosed in *Palestrina*. It is, however, precisely in this latter *magnum opus* of so outwardly and outspokenly conservative a composer as Pfitzner that I now wish to consider the disturbing relationship between progress and the courting of oblivion thus outlined by Mann and Adorno, in the effort to isolate some aspect of progress that might, after all, tend towards life and the future; that might relate to the positive strain in the multiple dualities that Mann referred to in his essay on *Palestrina* (where he observed of his prototype Hans Castorp: "He had to choose ... between duty and the service of life and fascination with death ...."[4]).

It is probably easiest to begin with the more negative and decadent aspect of *Palestrina,* whose weighty, post-Wagnerian *longueurs* have been frequently commented upon and have contributed much to the myth that the work can hold no interest for a non-German audience. Wagnerian it certainly is, however, in a quite specific musical sense that fully justifies Max Graf's observation in his eightieth-birthday tribute to the composer: "In a world grown unromantic, Pfitzner is the last Wagnerian."[5] But not only is it a question of Pfitzner's romantic idealism; the very way in which the text is set – some of the most inconsequential dialogue persists in eschewing Straussian realism and submits to the ponderous, even lugubrious will of the musical pace – has more in common with *Parsifal* than *Der Rosenkavalier.* The comparison with the former extends beyond matters of musical style. For where *Parsifal* not unintentionally turned out to be a wholly appropriate 'last work', *Palestrina* too seems to have been conceived from the outset as a terminal statement, and not only in Pfitzner's own career (which was in fact far from over). While the ostensible subject of the opera is the myth concerning Palestrina's inspired composition of the 'Pope Marcellus' Mass, whereby the Council of Trent was persuaded against a ban on polyphonic music in the Church, the actual drama (and the libretto was Pfitzner's own) revolves around the ageing artist who seems to have lost, along with his beloved wife, both his creative power and his sense of belonging to the world in which he finds himself. Only against all odds, and through reawakened veneration for the ancient masters of the tradition at whose latter end he himself stands, does

Palestrina become the vessel of divine inspiration once more. While the new mass effectively saves the great tradition for posterity, the conclusion of the opera finds Palestrina, having shunned the public acclaim being voiced noisily in the street below, greeting the twilight of his days with mystical acceptance as his absent-minded organ improvisation dwindles to a single held note that fades into the darkness as the curtain descends.

It is hardly surprising that Mann found more than mere "mimicry and historic atmosphere" in the "archaic fifths and fourths, these organ sonorities and church modes"[6] of the first and third acts. He was, however, somewhat taken aback when, in a summer evening's conversation at the time of the first performances of *Palestrina*, Pfitzner himself had contributed the following to a general comparison of his work with *Die Meistersinger* (no doubt inspired by parallels between the roles of Palestrina and Hans Sachs and the ceremonial aspect of *Palestrina's* second act's depiction of a chaotic session of the Council of Trent):

> The difference is most plainly expressed in the closing scenes. At the end of *Die Meistersinger* – a stage full of sunlight, rejoicing crowds, a betrothal, glitter and praise; in my work, Palestrina, honoured to be sure – alone in the twilight of his room, beneath the picture of his departed wife, at the organ, dreaming. The Meistersinger are the apotheosis of the new, heralds of the future of life; in *Palestrina* everything leans to the past; there is a prevailing sympathy with death.[7]

This last phrase was the very one that Mann himself

had used in the story that would turn into *The Magic Mountain,* and it appears unequivocally to demonstrate a spiritual decadence that throws into even sharper relief the manifest conservatism of the operatic technique and musical language employed. Yet we have only to glance back at the main criteria of Theodor Adorno's critical vindication of Schoenberg's 'progressive truth' to find *Palestrina* remarkably eligible for a similar vindication on almost every count. The work itself, through its manner and language, would in no way have alienated the bourgeois opera-audience of Munich in 1917: Pfitzner's music remains (in the language of *Doctor Faustus*) "per du" with humanity and thus permits *Palestrina* to express rather than merely illustrate graphically its conceptual, philosophical aspect. Nevertheless, it ingenuously offers the material for a case-study of its composer (both as an individual and as a product of his culture) who, in his manifest sympathy with the central character, rejects the coercive barbarism of modern mass society that is symbolized in the opera by the 'democratic' travesty of the Council of Trent's deliberations, that end in chaos and a blood-bath. No less than Schoenberg's "denial of the illusion of beauty" (to recall Adorno's diagnosis) does *Palestrina* manifest "the perception of misfortune...". The work's conclusion certainly looks towards a kind of oblivion that could render it the character of a "message of despair from the shipwrecked."[8]

★ ★ ★

If this equation of Schoenberg's so-called Progress with Pfitzner's so-called Conservatism seems to smack of sophistry, we would do well to recall that Pfitzner was very much a figure in the landscape of German music during the First World War and beyond. One of his many influential advocates was Alma Mahler – by that time the widow of one of the great pioneers of musical modernism and certainly not a lady to squander her attentions on irrelevant reactionaries. On more than one occasion in her two books of memoirs, she explains how Richard Strauss always struck her as somewhat of a worldling "between two musical pillar-saints, Pfitzner and Schoenberg".[9] A remarkable entry in her diary after a performance of Mahler's Seventh Symphony under Krauss in the winter of 1930–1 reads: "There is no clear-cut choice ... Whose way is right – the gloomy Mahler's or that of the lucid Richard Strauss? And what about Pfitzner? And Schoenberg? Probably all four are right, each in his way."[10]

One of the ways in which Pfitzner made his presence felt was as a prolific and frequently polemical writer on musical subjects. In 1920 he engaged in a celebrated public controversy with Alban Berg over the questions of musical inspiration and analysis.[11] A few years earlier, in fact in 1917, the very year in which *Palestrina* was first performed, he had initiated one with the composer and virtuoso pianist Ferruccio Busoni – a controversy that is of particular relevance to the present discussion, for the reason that it demonstrates with some clarity the extent to which Pfitzner was conscious both of his own position as evinced in *Palestrina* and of the bogus philosopy of the modernist, or what he loosely termed the "futuristic" credo with respect to matters of technical and linguistic "progress".

Specifically what occasioned his wrath was a little pamphlet by Busoni entitled *Entwurf einer neuen Aesthetik der Tonkunst* (Sketch of a New Aesthetic of Music),[12] the first version of which seems to have been published as early as 1906. It was republished by the Insel Verlag in 1910 and then, in its final version, in 1916 – the version that fell under the critical scrutiny of Pfitzner (it was also this edition in which Schoenberg made copious marginal notes).[13] As an Italian by birth, Busoni's writing was quite free of the darkly tortuous mystical strain that informs Schoenberg's literary style. Thus his New Aesthetic, deriving much of its tone, and a little of its philosophy, from Nietzsche's praise of the light-hearted south over the heavy Germanic north in his anti-Wagner polemics, presents with blithe, one might almost say naive clarity, a plea to composers to free themselves from all restrictions of the past as they soar towards an ideal art of unfettered nuance and unimagined forms – a perfect 'imitation of nature' that realizes music's truest aspect as a radiant child that *"floats on air!"*: "It touches not the earth with its feet. It knows no law of gravitation. It is wellnigh incorporeal. Its material is transparent. It is sonorous air. It is almost Nature herself. It is – free."[14]

But freedom, Busoni continues, "is something that mankind has never wholly comprehended, never realized to the full." To do so in music, we must renounce "routine" along with the sterile rules of harmony and counterpoint; we must renounce our hidebound system of notation, our twelve-degree octave and seven-degree scales. In short, as Pfitzner observes in the pamphlet he published in response (1917), Busoni's rosy dreams of the future perfectibility of the art "are inseparable from a negation (more hinted at than clearly stated) of all that has gone before."[15] Entitled '*Futuristengefahr*' (Danger of the Futurists), Pfitzner's essay resolutely refuses to join in Busoni's heady game of building aesthetic castles in the air. Just as the latter was quite justified in accusing Pfitzner, in a subsequent open letter to the *Süddeutsche Monatshefte*, of having misrepresented his book ("which is well-meant and full of peace . . ."[16]), so too was Pfitzner equally justified in taking a sober look at Busoni's rhapsodies and attempting to show as clearly as possible what they would appear to signify. Much of what he has to say about Busoni's rapturous rush into the future is fascinatingly relevant to the whole study of both modernist and anti-modernist theorizing in the twentieth century.

Through all the polemical lightning-flashes and ironic asides of Pfitzner's pamphlet, there looms one central article of faith to which much of the ensuing substance of his critique naturally relates. While not denying outright the possibility of an exciting and unexpected future for any art-form, Pfitzner holds to the belief that the *means* of artistic expression develop in accordance with changes in what artists feel that they have to say; with the nature of their 'inspiration' (in German: *Einfall*). To suggest that artists, rather than creating stylistic norms, are in fact hampered by them – as Busoni certainly does – is, Pfitzner implies, to make a rather elementary kind of philosophical error, which in Busoni's case relates to a confusion of artistic and scientific modes of progress. While specific goals may be set in science – the solution of specific problems aimed at – "Art has no mission and no goals":

> Each work of art is a world in itself. . . . Not art, but the *artist* has a goal: namely to make the best possible use of the gift that has been bestowed upon him. . . . The greatness and perfection of art depends not upon the greatness and perfection of the means, but of the artist.[17]

Having established that the future end of Busoni's "striving-after-goals" (*Zielstrebigkeit*)[18] can be conceived in no other fashion than as an insubstantial poetic intimation (a "deeply portentous chamber in which the holy-of-holies is supposed to be found"[19]), Pfitzner indicates that the only kind of progress that could interest him in the sphere of art would have to concern the human heart – the mind and *spirit* of the artist whose technical and formal innovations may naturally follow from his struggle to articulate a new kind of *Einfall*. To try, as it were, to coax the *Einfall* by concentrating first on the technical innovation, on 'emancipating the dissonance' or, in Busoni's case, on dividing the limiting tone into third- and sixth-tones, is to put the cart before the horse and produce a new kind of Kitsch; what Pfitzner calls "Futuristic-Kitsch":

> This variety differs from its brethren in that it pleases no one, not even the futurists . . . [who]

certainly do not see art as something to be enjoyed. Unswervingly, never seeing a joke, these
unfortunate delivery-men drag towards us in the
sweat of their brows the material of future crea-
tions, future creators, of which they know
nothing.[20]

All great art, Pfitzner observes, is in reality unique
and has in its own way reached that very goal whose
gaining Busoni would appear to regard as impossible
save that we discard the past and, by adopting a
cranky kind of idealism, pin all our hopes upon some
'yet-to-be' that can only be defined in terms of what
now 'is not'. Polemical as his essay is, Pfitzner holds
back from suggesting in so many words that Busoni's
artistic millenialism is but the dangerously misleading
outward face of inner emptiness, but repeatedly expresses his extreme suspicion of that kind of portentous newness that is as comprehensively impene-
trable to him as "the music of some wild tribe or the
musical language of thousands of years ago".[21] (After
all, none of his innovating contemporaries were wild
tribesmen or thousands of years old). Towards the end
of his essay, Pfitzner lays his own cards on the table
with respect to that shining future for whose sake we
are so comprehensively to free ourselves:

> What if it were otherwise, however? ... What if
> our last century or century-and-a-half re-
> presented the flowering of Western music, the
> climax, the real golden age, which will never
> return and which is now passing into decline, into
> a state of decadence, as after the age of Greek
> tragedy? My own feelings incline rather more to
> this view.[22]

Suspecting that the task of his own time might, after all, be to permit "a loving reflection upon what has been and what is now happening", Pfitzner nevertheless understood well the bullying fashionableness of the futuristic manner: "Previously the question was asked of everything New: Am I comfortable about that, do I understand it? Nowadays it is rather: Am I going to make a fool of myself by being conservative?"[23] In concluding, he bitterly (and yet presciently with respect to Schoenberg's greatest unfinished work!) turns the tables upon the antiacademic Busoni, taunting him not least with the prototype electronic instrument whose invention he celebrates in the *New Aesthetic*:

> If the period of time that links Bach, Beethoven and Wagner with the present really represents a supreme climax of the development of our beloved art, then we have also to thank in due measure the conscientious application and the brilliant achievement throughout the century of the theoreticians and teachers. Far more deserving than these least deserving of impoverished Masters might we call – *Busoni* a 'lawgiver'. He is the futuristic Moses who shows his adepts the promised land.... Thou shalt not write in existing forms! I am Mr Thaddeus Cahill's Dynamophone: thou shalt have no other musical instrument but me![24]

Is there not in fact, he continues, an evasively cold side to Busoni, that has even a specifically suicidal aspect? For does not Busoni's sense of being restricted by bar-lines and other notational conventions, by harmonic practice and established formal types, corres-

pond to a kind of existential anguish at the fact that
night always follows day, that every minute of our
lives we "must purchase with a breath"? "A man
would hang himself if such conditions were to prevail.
Our aesthetician similarly wants music to commit
suicide; it remains to be seen whether it will be healthy
enough not to do it."[25] Pfitzner himself goes on to
suggest that maybe it would be better if music *were* to
end, if Busoni's implied picture of its present state is
true; if the art indeed represents no more than "a
neglected tract of land where plants grow wild and go
to seed in untended soil, a few partly crumbled stones
marking the graves of heroes, between which oc-
casional wooden signposts point into the blue."[26] Only
in Pfitzner's emphasized and separated final sentence
(*"And all around there stretch beautiful green pastures."*[27]) is there sounded a renewed note of hope in
the suggestion that Busoni has, after all, been doing no
more than looking fixedly down at his own feet.

★ ★ ★

There is no doubt that in one sense the *Futuristengefahr* confirms and underlines our reading of the
decadent and terminal aspect of *Palestrina*. Yet
Pfitzner, in his old-fashioned, argumentatively pedantic way, really does little more than anticipate
Adorno's later and more philosophically searching
reduction of the technical aspects of musical modernism to a tragic function of despair in an age whose

greatest truth was to be found beyond the cold labyrinths of 'progressive art' in a willing silence. But
where Adorno sees necessity, Pfitzner sees danger, and
it is indeed precisely at this point, when we question
the ultimate truth and inevitability of this apparently
pathological darkness of the spirit and the attendant
onset of a new expressive ice age, that *Palestrina*
proves so richly interesting. Let us reconsider first its
darkest aspect as both symptom and victim of that
tragic but authentically modern despair referred to
above; of that decadent "spiritual inclination and
intellectual disposition" which Thomas Mann had
initially welcomed (in 1918) as "the opposite of a
politically virtuous inclination and temperament."[28]
Here it is that we may treat its content as the material
for a 'case-study' (in the broadly psychoanalytic sense
in which Adorno approvingly applies the term to
Schoenberg's expressionistic works).

To consider first the matter of *political* evil embraced by the opera, we need only look more closely at
the events of Act II, which Pfitzner himself regarded
as a "picture of the hectic tumult of the outside world
which is hostile to the still creative work of the genius
and could only be represented by the Council."[29] It
has been pointed out elsewhere[30] that the implications
of the chaos that breaks out in the Council's deliberations are plainly anti-democratic (democratic discussion fails because the various national factions have
their own political axes to grind, just as ambition, folly
or general cynicism prompts the individual protagonists and spokesmen). Palestrina himself makes no
appearance in this act, of course, and one might put it

that in his stead Pfitzner finds his own representative in Cardinal Madruscht – the 'German' host to this final meeting of the Council who is described on his entry as being a "powerfully built man, who, despite his ecclesiastical robes, gives more the impression of a warrior, a nobleman."[31] Casting a cynical eye over the proceedings from the outset, Madruscht takes relatively little part in the action until, in those extraordinary final moments of Act II, he appears with his guards and, his exasperation at last finding an outlet, has mercilessly gunned down on stage the brawling rabble of Spanish versus German and Italian servants and street urchins who were, after all, only following their masters' example, if with their fists rather than with verbal slander. There can be little question that Madruscht, an idealistic, romantic German knight beneath his Cardinal's robes, represents what in the nationalistic Pfitzner was dangerously in accord with that element in his society that would shortly replace democratic inoperancy with Fascist intolerance. How interesting it is that this Act should be introduced by an orchestral prelude that contains the most advanced and 'modern' music in the opera – the extraordinary Shostakovich-like fracas of the opening (with its motor rhythms and stuttering brass ejaculations) giving way to the expansive Straussian manner in splendid fashion.

Considered in the light of this second act, it is hardly surprising that the opera should have so fascinated Thomas Mann that he attended five performances of it in 1917, the year of its Munich première. For even though he himself still harboured the sentiments of a 'Romantic' German patriotism at this time, he in no way failed to register the fact that one of the most ambivalent themes of his own art was here embodied in the very structure of Pfitzner's opera, where two acts celebrating artistic idealism are joined by a third that appears to justify social barbarism. How problematically modern a work *Palestrina* indeed was! And how appropriate it is that the third act should be so markedly lacking in new musical inspiration after the garish splendours of the second; that it should so comprehensively exhibit the characteristics of a weary epilogue to the whole, where the atmosphere of antique Gothic piety, touched here and there by the echoes of long-ago hymns, hangs like autumn mist in the cloisters of a deserted monastery. All seems heavy with sleep and sunset solemnity. The brief appearance of the Pope himself, come to congratulate and honour the composer of the 'saving' mass, goes for nothing musically, and even the distantly cheery music of the celebrating crowd fails convincingly to introduce a new mood. Palestrina has had the fact of his necessary distance from the world violently impressed upon him in the form of the imprisonment he has suffered at the hands of the however contrite Borromeo. All that he has to say in this shortest of the opera's three acts tends towards the concluding prayer (from which, in fact, the whole work seems to have grown in Pfitzner's imagination) in which he welcomes a peaceful decline in the hope that the closing of the ring of his own existence will be fashioned aright by God. Music itself seems consigned to the past as the curtain falls upon that single, fading organ D that quite gives the lie to the glib notion, sometimes voiced, that Pfitzner regarded *Palestrina* as *his* Pope Marcellus Mass. Even the divine dictation of the Mass by the heavenly host towards the end of Act I has rather the effect of a transitory *recollection* of Mahler's Eighth Symphony.

★ ★ ★

We might imagine that *Palestrina* is indeed, in the terms of the *Futuristengefahr,* given over entirely to a "loving reflection upon what has been". Precisely at this juncture might we wonder anew whether it would, after all, be best now to freeze the sick soul within the icy labyrinths of a new kind of posthumous art, in the ascetic rigours of whose constructional aspect artistic technique itself is at least preserved in aspic (to modify Adorno's suggestion) for unimaginable banquets of the future. But Pfitzner, who in all other respects than his compositional technique and musical language seems to have kept as firmly abreast of the times as his more zealously 'futuristic' breathren (however allergic his narrow chest may have been to the "air of other planets"), plays what he may well have believed to be a trump card in *Palestrina* – one that he had himself described in the *Futuristengefahr* when commenting upon the self-sufficiency of artistic inspiration; upon the essential irresponsibility of art (which has no goals other than those it realizes in itself, we recall) and the nature of the sympathetic communication between artist and audience. Not for nothing, after all, does his essay conclude with a timely reminder of the "beautiful green pastures" that surround us, would we but see them.

For all that I may have said about the retrospective aspect of the angels' song, it is precisely during and after the revelatory climax of Act I that these pastures open before us. They do so in a fashion that returns us to the aspect of *Palestrina* as psychoanalytic 'case-study' – but in this instance the case-study of a dynamic process of healing and renewal. The magic begins at the point where the weary and sad composer has in no uncertain terms rejected the pat demands of society, that come here in the form of Borromeo's request for an exemplary mass to bring before the Council. He refuses to prostitute his talent and prod-uce a hack-work – for that is all he could do, now that his heart has been broken by the death of his wife, his spirits saddened by the strange new ways that have so captivated the imagination of his pupil Silla, whose impending defection to Florence is in no way compen-sated for by the faithful adherence of his son Ighino:

> ... I'm weak and full of failings,
> and as for progress, nothing's left for me.
> I am an old man, weary unto death,
> part of an age that's coming to an end.
> Before me I see nothing else but sorrow –
> and can wring nothing more out of my soul.

These words are not uttered to Borromeo, however, who has long since stormed off to Trent, scenting heresy in Palestrina's rejection of a holy duty. They are elicited rather by the spirits of the ancient masters of sacred music who gather to take up the threads of Borromeo's abandoned persuasion, as all pretence of historical reconstruction gives way to naive fantasy in the section of the opera that earns it its sub-title of *Musical Legend*. Even the ancient masters, however, fail to persuade Palestrina of his divinely ordained duty to provide the crowning work of their tradition and "give meaning to this age". Instead, his nihilism grows apace at their insistence upon his fulfilling his "earthly mission":

> Why this whole game – Apart from this what would there be? – Why this whole game?

They do not answer, but shortly leave, having vouchsafed him no more than an enigmatic description of the "age-old Master of the world who has no name":

> ... who's likewise subject
> to the primeval word on the brink of eternity.
> He does his work, as you do yours,
> he forges rings, and images, and precious stones,
> for the shining chain of the ages
> and of everything in the world.

Thus deserted by even these encouraging shades, Palestrina expresses terror in the darkest depths of the symbolic night that engulfs him. It is here, by virtue of its very naiveté, that Pfitzner's fantasy reveals most in its previously mentioned aspect as case-study in spiritual regeneration. Even as he gives vent to his fear and thus lays himself open at the moment of his greatest agony ("Alone in deepest darkness, wretched and terrified, I raise my voice to Heaven") Palestrina is unknowingly visited by a gathering throng of angels who give voice to the hymn of praise that he now, in growing rapture, writes down as the Mass that he had hitherto refused to compose. The "eternal song of praise" becomes one with the "Mystery of love" as his dead wife's voice joins with those of the angels:

> Through the deepness of night,
> through joy in my genius,
> I feel united
> with blessed mankind. . . .

For Palestrina the moment of ecstatic revelation passes. The natural chemistry of the spirit has effected a resolution of the inner conflict and, in the magical time-scale of the legend, the Mass is completed in the twinkling of an eye. As the vision fades, Palestrina drops his pen and falls asleep. Yet it is precisely at this point that the heart of Pfitzner's *Einfall* is revealed to us. A metaphysical conflict also has been resolved: in mythical terms by Palestrina's act of human *expression* and in present creative terms by Pfitzner's submission to the dictates of egocentric fantasy. By becoming thus creatively childlike once again, the ancient rift between man and nature is healed and Pfitzner too gives way to a hymn of world-love in the extraordinary dawn that now fills the theatre with morning light and the sound of the bells of Rome tolling in majestic procession. A simple whole-tone oscillation, like a mysterious under-tow from the preceding waves of revelation, slowly gathers in power and breadth until, resplendent with deep bells and tam-tam, it generates a great paean of trumpeting glory that returns, after the brief morning discovery by Silla and Ighino of Palestrina's strewn pages, to conclude the act in a peroration that encompasses something of the epic awe of Sibelius coupled with the jubilation of Janáček.

The mood never returns. In the profounder sense, Pfitzner was certainly too rigorously modern and realistic a composer to end his opera in anything other than the darkness that follows another sunset, and in the historically fateful key of D minor. Yet that moment remains with us when, some two hours later, we leave the theatre less burdened by despair than warmed by the recollection, at least, of a life-affirming revelation (the capacity for which, Pfitzner had observed in the *Futuristengefahr*, "man can only derive from *art*"[32]). For in Europe's autumn, in the third year of the First World War, Pfitzner the testy old conservative, touched in no uncertain terms with the German malaise, had erected a signpost towards precisely that kind of spiritual or even psychological progress whose elusiveness is otherwise bitterly registered in *Palestrina*, as it was reflected in the hermetic exercises in abnegation of the futuristic innovators. They, however, appeared deludingly to project on to a distant future the goal that Pfitzner, with much more disturbing rigour, located in the recent past. Perhaps, when viewed in this light, we can begin to sympathize with *Palestrina's* first conductor, Bruno Walter, who considered the opera "the mightiest musical-dramatic work of our time",[33] just as Thomas Mann found it in accord with his "innermost idea of humanity" to the extent that he could draw from it the reassurance to resume at last his own war-interrupted creative work.[34]

EIGHT

Schreker's Decline

... this style was penetrating and sickly, tense
and subtle, careful to record the intangible impression that affects the senses and produces feeling, and skilled in modulating the complicated
nuances of an epoch that was itself extraor-
dinarily complex. It was, in fact, the sort of style
that is indispensable to decrepit civilizations
which, in order to express their needs, and to
whatever age they may belong, require new ac-
ceptations, new uses, new forms both of word
and phrase.[1]

This description of the literary style of Edmond de
Goncourt itself appears in a work of fiction: that
strange document of decadent taste and sensibility, *À
Rebours* by Joris-Karl Huysmans. Some of this novel's
subsequent notoriety (it was first published in 1884)
stemmed from the fact that it played a part in Oscar
Wilde's *The Picture of Dorian Gray*, whose hero found
it "a poisonous book. The heavy odour of incense
seemed to cling about its pages and to trouble the
brain. The mere cadence of the sentences, the subtle
monotony of their music ... produced in the mind ...

a form of reverie, a malady of dreaming ...".[2] The impression it makes upon Dorian Gray is misleading, however. He seems to read it entirely as if it were one of the volumes in its protagonist's own library; for Huysmans certainly leaves us in no doubt that Duc Jean Floressas des Esseintes was possessed of a literary and artistic taste whose refinement permitted him to recognize "only such works as had been sifted and distilled by subtle and tormented minds ...".[3]

In fact *À Rebours* documents and analyses the avowedly decadent taste of Des Esseintes in a manner whose underlying self-consciousness renders it as much a satire as the scented and perverse indulgence that its reputation suggests. By the end of the book we realize that Des Esseintes' flight from reality into a world of aesthetic artifice, however extreme its manifestations, has been prompted by critical perceptions *about* that reality, and the society that supported it, that could equally well have led him to Karl Marx as to Verlaine, Mallarmé and Goncourt. Indeed that could well be his next move, for the end of the novel finds him ironically denied the nervously disruptive pleasures of his aesthetic retreat and condemned by the doctors – for the sake of his health – to return to that very reality from whose debased, bourgeois mediocrity he had sought to escape.

The potent but ambivalent solace of art was a theme revived in European literature well before Thomas Mann made of it a favourite subject of his own works, whose romantic heritage and Nietzschean parentage led him much more readily than Huysmans to seek in music, and specifically *modern* music, the most appropriate object of decadent taste. Huysmans himself perceived that there was something inconsistent about Des Esseintes' musical asceticism (his passion is for plainsong, for all that he loves Schubert) and puts this down to his fastidious dislike of the promiscuously social side of music. Des Esseintes, who is only a tolerable pianist, observes of modern secular music that it cannot be enjoyed in the privacy of one's home. His disinclination to sweat in the midst of a theatrical mob is the sole reason, we are given to understand, for his lack of any real knowledge of Berlioz or "the mighty Wagner operas".[4] Certainly the few modern French writers whose works Des Esseintes allows into his library (Baudelaire, Verlaine, Mallarmé and the like) had fewer scruples in this matter and were much drawn to music as a model for their own aesthetic experiments, as they would in their turn provide both inspiration and material for that great French composer in whom Des Esseintes, suitably furnished with a modern gramophone, might have found much to his taste – namely Debussy.

That Debussy's literary inspiration is documented in advance with uncanny accuracy in Chapter XIV of *À Rebours* (including specific discussion of Mallarmé's *Faune* and the "morbid psychology" of Edgar Allan Poe) is a fact that could well lead to a consideration of the decadent aspect of his music. Current music-historical fashion nevertheless decrees that he be considered primarily in his role as iconoclastic pioneer and innovator – and particularly by those who, with good cause, would seek some alternative 'founder of modern music' to either the tortured Schoenberg or the brilliantly chilly Stravinsky. The reverse holds true of the German opera composer Franz Schreker (1878–1934), who was much compared with Debussy in his lifetime and unquestionably regarded as a brave pioneer of modernism. Yet his name has now all but disappeared from the history books, and when he *is* mentioned it is precisely as an exemplar of that regressive, 'decadent' style of which Schoenberg is supposed heroically to have purged himself after *Pelleas* and the *Gurrelieder* (of which work Schreker was the appropriate first conductor).

If we use Huysmans' description of Goncourt's literary style as a guide, there is no question but that much of Schreker's musical output could be pressed into service as an example of that extreme kind of decadence that was courted and toyed with – sometimes as no more than an idea or a wicked intimation – by writers of the *fin de siècle*. The prelude to his once popular opera *Die Gezeichneten* (completed in 1915) could be used as an excellent example of all those traits familiarly attributed to the most authentic image of artistic decadence: it is sensuous in an unashamed and indeed unbridled way that would merit the epithet 'indulgent'; it is highly complex in its wealth of decorative elaboration that recalls the effect of Beardsley's most elaborate drawings; it rejoices in techniques of tonal, harmonic and melodic ambivalence that gives its surface an iridescent shimmer in which it is difficult to distinguish the light from the shade; it does not significantly 'progress' but materializes like a strange dream out of a state of drugged, semi-conscious torpor into which it finally dissolves once more at its end. One might go on, but the point is made. The piece, in short, rejoices in that kind of irresponsible aesthetic beauty that seems to renounce both morality and rationality in the way that the paintings of Gustave Moreau appeared to do for Des Esseintes, who found in them "subtle, exquisite refinement, steeped in an atmosphere of ancient fantasy, wrapped in an aura of antique corruption, divorced from modern times and modern society."[5]

Suddenly we seem to have chanced upon a textbook case of the fabled disease that required such stringent and extreme remedies for the survival of modern music – and an example of the disease that reveals its true nature as a moral, spiritual and even psychological one before ever it infected harmonic progressions and the very foundations of the language of nineteenth-century music (if we are to believe the history books). The fact that Schreker never finally or systematically renounced the full affective vocabulary of that language is what gives his often highly expressionistic style so radically different a character from Schoenberg's. There is the same waywardness and fragmentation of the material, the unexpected constantly surprising us in the form of frustrating evasions, of nervous withdrawals of half-made statements, of sudden shocks and mysterious little ostinati that come and go like unbidden, ghostly 'extras' in a threatening dream. Yet Schoenberg's will-less stream of nervous activity is reduced to hard, abstract data that can be read with scientific objectivity (for all that it is in reality a highly wilful, graphic caricature of the *idea* of the Freudian unconscious). Schreker's, on the other hand, is indeed a stream of *consciousness* in the most profound sense – for we recognize the progressions that have been interrupted, we respond to the manner of the haunted 'recollection' (even of something we have never heard) and suffer the dissonances as intentionally painful in their broad context of tonal consonance.

The more one looks at Schreker's music for clarification of what it was that his more authentically 'modern', Second-Viennese-School contemporaries purged themselves of, the more interesting does it appear; the more quickly do the orthodoxies of the history books prove propagandistic fables of mysterious origin. This, of course, is my point. Just as Nietzsche failed to perceive the full significance of *Parsifal*; just as Dorian Gray failed to analyse Huysmans' purpose in *À Rebours*, so have the historians of twentieth-century music spent so much time coming to terms with the problematic surface of Schoenberg, Berg and Webern, that they have, almost inevitably, neglected the equally problematic *content* of such an apparently decadent stylistic conservative as Schreker.

* * *

The prelude to *Die Gezeichneten* might, then, readily illustrate to the uninitiated what Alma Mahler meant when she once described Schreker as a breeder of

"hot-house fantasies",[6] or why his music has been
associated with the decorative preoccupations of the
Viennese *Jugendstil*; with painters like Klimt and
dramatists like Gerhardt Hauptmann and Strindberg.
He studied in Vienna at precisely the right time, and
even scored his first major success as a composer at the
Secessionist Kunstschau of 1908 with the ballet-
pantomime *Der Geburtstag der Infantin* – based on
Oscar Wilde. The very subject matter of *Die
Gezeichneten*, which is set in Renaissance Genoa and
deals in orgies, corruption and crippled artists, seems
to confirm our suspicions that Schreker, had he not
existed, might almost have been created by Thomas
Mann in a maliciously whimsical draft for *Doctor
Faustus*. The plot thickens, however, when we read
what Schreker himself had to say about the opera,
namely that "the collapse of Germany, even the decline of our culture, is clearly presaged, like the writing on the wall, in the music and in the degenerate
character of this work."[7]

Clearly, then, Schreker's decadent 'self-indulgence'
has another more self-conscious aspect, just as had
Huysmans' notorious novel and so much other 'merely' decadent art of the period. We might be inclined
to see his musical world as diametrically opposed to
that of Mahler, in which the spirit of traditional
European humanism made a last great effort to balance heroic conscience and consciousness against post-
Freudian despair. The painful rationale of Mahler's
inexorable counterpoint, that sings its way upwards
through the potentially uncontrollable chaos of the
music's inner affective life, disappears from Schreker's

music along with the possibility of true symphonic form which could permit itself the illusion of an argued or symbolically achieved conclusion. However, it is in the implications of the remarkable, if somewhat undisciplined libretti, that Schreker himself wrote for all of his operas from *Der ferne Klang* onwards, that the other side of the Mahlerian equation is to be found. The music itself may have sunk beneath the waves of the unconscious, but Schreker's curious symbolic dramas prove to evince as lively a comprehension as Thomas Mann's of all that stemmed from Nietzsche's reservations about Wagner's Germanic interpretation of the role of Romantic Artist.

The hero of *Die Gezeichneten* (The Marked Ones) could almost be a caricature, in the style of Mann, of such a romantic artist. He is an ugly and crippled young nobleman, named Alviano Salvago. Denied the normal pleasures of life, he creates a paradise-island of aesthetic artifice ("Elysium") which he never visits himself, but which his more fortunately endowed friends use as a secret venue for unbridled orgies, for the purpose of which they kidnap Genoa's fairest daughters. In a belated attempt to expiate their crimes, however, the creator of Elysium throws it open to the general public. Not only are its delights all too much for *them*; it is precisely at the height of the opening celebrations on the island that the one woman Alviano thought to have returned his love is ravished to the point of death by one of his handsome young friends. What is more, she enjoyed every moment, and reveals as much as she dies, to the elemental anguish of Alviano. As a painter (with a weak heart) she had really been interested in him only as an artistic subject!

It will be clear from this very brief synopsis that Schreker's libretti are no less prone than his music to go over the top. His lack of self-criticism or willingness to submit his works to revision and pruning were elements in the gathering critical opposition of the later 1920s which, when it came to be manipulated by Nazi propagandists in the early 1930s, set the seal on his downfall and not indirectly brought about his death from a stroke in 1934. But Paul Bekker once pointed out[8] that Wagner's libretti frequently make no less awkward an impression when considered apart from the musical context that makes sense of them – and which in Schreker's case avowedly formed the starting-point of his inspiration: "I work from the music..." he said; "My initial ideas are more musical than literary. The mysteriously inward struggles for musical expression."[9]

That is, of course, a profoundly romantic attitude: one that implicitly alludes to the whole tradition of German romantic thought that had accorded a portentous and revelatory role to music above all the arts precisely because it sprang from sources that were not altogether rationally apprehensible. And yet, the burden of Nietzsche's criticism of Wagner was that these mysterious sources were growing all *too* apprehensible as Schopenhauer's grand, inchoate Will revealed itself precisely as a drift of mental and emotional energy that presented in fact no more than the image of a wholly inner world defined by the artist's psychopathology. That Schreker's "mysteriously inward" is in fact to be interpreted in a Freudian light is made abundantly clear in more or less all of his operatic libretti, from *Der ferne Klang* onwards, in which Music itself (conceived traditionally as the highest manifestation of the business of Art) plays a remarkable role: invested once more with all the ambivalence with which it had commanded the awed respect of the ancient Greeks or the early Church Fathers, but interpreted in a thoroughly modern fashion.

Der ferne Klang itself (completed in 1910) is in one sense an indulgent post-Wagnerian opera, for all its social realism and the frequently expressionistic modernity of its lyrical style – traits which are often seen as prophetic of *Wozzeck* (and it should be remembered that Berg produced the first version of the vocal score of *Der ferne Klang*). Yet its message is that art leads the aspiring young composer Fritz away from life like a kind of counterfeit *Ewigweibliche*. The 'distant sound' entices him *away* from his beloved Grethe and is directly responsible for her descent into a life of prostitution. Furthermore, the snatches of Fritz's opera that we hear in Act III make it clear that it is indeed *Der ferne Klang*, the opera we are watching (if disguised under the title, *Die Harfe*, that Schreker had originally conceived for his own work). The work is a Romantic opera in a sense that would have been well understood by E. T. A. Hoffmann and his contemporaries, certain as they were of the need both to create and break illusions. The distant sound that lures Fritz away in the first act is a magical siren song that seems to him somehow bound up with the mysteries of Nature. Only in the third act does he really attend to

Nature (in the extraordinary dawn-chorus scene) and at the same time understand that that other sound of his youth had been generated from within himself by his love for the girl he left behind.

With *Das Spielwerk und die Prinzessin* (completed in 1912) we leave realism behind altogether and descend into the wholly 'musical' realm of a fantastically evoked medieval world of castles and princesses. Yet precisely at the centre of this fantasy world do we encounter the first of those symbolic representations of Music itself that appear in a number of his later works. Here it is the mysterious *Spielwerk* created by old Meister Florian: a kind of mechanical carillon that once produced magical music but is now mysteriously silent. Its creator is not to be confused with the aspiring artist of *Der ferne Klang*, however. He is rather the originator of the mysterious sound whose nature and identity Fritz had longed to discover. Meister Florian stands ostensibly for neither good nor evil, although he has significantly disowned his wife and son, who had permitted the wicked princess to use the magic power of the carillon to inspire and enhance her drunken orgies. Consistent with the gradual metamorphosis of the Will in the post-Schopenhauerian intellectual tradition to which I have referred, the ambivalent mystery of music is here explicitly associated with the equally ambivalent mystery of the sexual libido. *Its* representative is the princess of the opera's title, who is quite as beautiful and quite as wicked as Salome – a nihilistic hedonist who is clearly given to reading modern novels. Her saviour is the innocent boy who wanders into her domain playing on a flute whose melodies, generated by the simple idealism of youth, prove to have the power to set the mysterious carillon playing once more.

The climax of the work takes the form of a wildly orgiastic festival that the princess has staged as the setting for her own theatrically conceived self-destruction (prompted by a mixture of self-loathing and sexual frustration). The forces of Dionysus are in fact unleashed so comprehensively that its climax finds her under immediate threat of being torn to pieces by an incensed mob of her simple subjects. But if the chaos proves here the very stuff of late-Romantic music, so also is it quelled by music: by the pure and radiant tones of the boy's flute. The forces of Apollo and Dionysus thus balanced, all join in a joyful dance of life, during which the princess leads the boy away to her castle. But a grim moral is registered in the final scene of the opera (which was given a more consolatory 'happy ending' when revised as *Das Spielwerk* in 1919).

The conception of this scene seems to have represented the primary inspiration for the whole work.[10] It begins at the point where the sound of the flute, whose music has once again set the mysterious carillon playing, is joined by a ghostly counterpoint from the fiddle of Meister Florian's recently dead son – the rapacious princess's former lover and victim. It would appear that Schreker chanced one evening upon a newspaper report of a famous violinist who had returned to his native village in Spain and, from a balcony, had serenaded far into the night a large crowd of its grateful inhabitants who had come to his house bearing torches. What Schreker seems to have conceived was a truly Hoffmannesque inversion of this charming picture of simple folk in the thrall of great art. *What if they had brought their torches to burn down the house and silence those dangerously magical sounds for ever?* Thus the opera ends with a group of townsfolk setting fire to Meister Florian's house and the strange carillon. The first of Schreker's characteristic theatrical immolations silences the mysterious source of music, leaving a smoking stage, the sound of a tolling bell and a stammered communal prayer.

★ ★ ★

The ambivalence and fate of the symbolic representations of Schreker's art grew clearer in implication as his work progressed. In *Der Schatzgräber* (completed in 1918) the minstrel's magic lute tracks down glittering treasure like a kind of metal-detector, but is equally drawn to human sorrow and misery, to which it must needs give expression (and the minstrel is interestingly as prone as Schreker to 'go too far', in that he is so readily carried away by his own singing that his narrative ballads tend to reveal all too much of the truth and precipitate new crises in the dramatic action). In *Irrelohe* (1924), the nuptial fiddler is constitutionally ineffectual in life and can only wreak his revenge upon it in a hatred that manifests itself characteristically in the fire with which he consumes

Irrelohe castle and with which he would destroy the power of human lust.

If there is sounded a note of hope in the possibility of life and love at the end of *Irrelohe*, it is a hope that looks beyond the machinations and devices of art. Certainly, in *Der singende Teufel* (completed in 1927), music was to find its most potently ambivalent symbolic form in his operas: in the great monastic organ whose builder had been burned as a magician. Although its completer, the builder's son Amandus, attempts to add to the daemonic character of its voicing angelic registers of love and benediction, the completed instrument is mercilessly used by the monks as a secret weapon with which to quell and subdue the life-affirming pagan folk who would destroy the monastery and who justifiably fear the great organ as a 'singing devil' (it is indeed literally the instrument of their carnage at the climax of the work). Once again, sensuality and judicious repression fail to find a way of living together in harmony and the pagan Lilian can only express her love for the monk Amandus by destroying the instrument he helped to create and which stands as a symbol of his guilt. She helps set fire to the monastery and burns beneath the great organ that emits its most angelic tones only as it melts in white heat.

But although the musical style of *Der singende Teufel* is already drastically chastened in many respects (austere linear polyphony begins to oust the clouds of harmonic alchemy), Schreker had already lost his lifelong battle with the critics. At the point where he had accomplished the remarkable feat of remaining a problematic modern composer who had achieved a real and indeed staggering popular success, he found himself no longer numbered among the *Neutöner*, but relegated to the shelf of regressive musical has-beens. It was in many respects not a surprising turn of events, for there was some justification in the critical verdict that already in *Irrelohe* Schreker had begun to tread water (although it contains some of his most searingly beautiful music). What is remarkable is the way in which his subsequent self-questioning led to what might have been a complete transformation of his style and approach, had he lived to realize the implications of his last opera, *Der Schmied von Gent* (1932). It is not in that work, however, but in the extraordinary *Christophorus* (completed in 1929) that Schreker's increasingly painful, almost schizophrenic ambivalence towards the very nature of the art-form to which he had devoted his life finds its most remarkable terminal statement.

Dedicated to Schoenberg, with whom Schreker had detailed discussions about the work,[11] *Christophorus* (which was not performed during his lifetime) is subtitled *Vision einer Oper ('Vision of an Opera')*. It takes the form of a highly original musical drama about the composition of an opera that should never have been; for Anselm, the modern protagonist, had been set by his teacher, Meister Johann, the task of writing a programmatic string quartet on the legend of St Christopher. However, he senses dramatic potential in the story of the man who sought to serve the greatest of all powers and who, having tried first the Emperor and then the Devil, had embarked upon a fruitless search for Christ. This he had finally abandoned for a life of service to others, bearing travellers across a river, until the increasing burden of a little child one day drowns him – the child being Christ, who names the dying man 'Christophorus' – bearer of Christ. Anselm sets himself the task of updating the legend, adding the necessary love-interest and having his modern Christopher serve first Art, specifically music of course, and then Love, before growing disillusioned with that too and, having shot his wife, plunging into an existential crisis that leads him to spiritualism and drugs.

As a sequel and coda to *Der singende Teufel*, and in a sense the whole of Schreker's previous output, *Christophorus* is in two particular respects disarmingly consistent and profoundly relevant to the most problematic obsessions of early twentieth-century art. In the first place, ultimate redemption is vouchsafed by the simple, trustingly innocent gaze of a little child – in fact the *son* of the struggling artist–Faust, Christoph. In the second we find that, having ritually burned the symbolic instrument of nineteenth-century music in *Der singende Teufel*, and indeed purged himself of many of the excesses of his own earlier style, Schreker now questions the very validity of opera.

An early sketch for the libretto clearly reveals that the work was initially concerned with the dualistic aspect of modern music – and it should be explained that the student composer Anselm casts himself as Christoph's friend and fellow artist, as well as rival in love, in his envisioned opera. He thus confronts his *alter ego* on stage, as reality and fantasy proceed together and grow dangerously entwined. Christophorus the musician wants, in this early draft, to bestow upon the world a "new art – an art of simplicity, born of a strong heart"; but his more successful opponent outdoes him with music that takes the form of "a hellish laughter . . . sprung from a people's shame and despair . . . convulsive rhythms, languishing melodies, a troubled soul, grotesquely deformed; the dance of the disinherited, the broken, the tortured – weeping laughter, the gambolling of Death . . .".[12] Already we see in this opposition the outward aspect of an internal conflict within Schreker's own creative personality – the master of the decadent style longing, like so many other Europeans in the 1920s, to become as a child again.

In the final version of *Christophorus*, the fictional hero is less explicit in his musical aims, which even in the First Act he publicly renounces in favour of Love: specifically love for the beautiful girl who is in fact Anselm's own beloved Lisa, the daughter of Meister Johann. The pain of her apparently heartless rejection of him in real life is assuaged by her ready submission to his "wishful creation", Christoph (for all that he intends to cast her with ironic bitterness as the temptress – the 'devil' of the piece). Yet as the imagined opera takes over the action of the real one, things start to go wrong in the realm of idealistic fantasy. Lisa has a child, hates her subsequent appearance and rejects her new role as mother and housewife. She also grows bored with the saintly Christoph and begins to incline once more to Anselm (in his imaginary role in his own opera). Christoph grows jealous of his creator and shoots Lisa, thus consigning himself to a new life of psychological torment as a fugitive. Gathering up all the threads of Schreker's operatic preoccupations, Christoph suffers unspeakably (in the most modern manner) on Anselm's behalf. In fact he takes on the burden of suffering to the extent that Anselm is moved, in compassion, to turn guardian and friend of his own creation, with whom he had previously been growing a little bored. A new sense of responsibility informs the agonized psychic dualism of the remainder of the opera, to the point where, begged by his dying child, Christoph literally turns out the lights in the theatre – the orchestra pit also is plunged into darkness – and retreats from the greedy gaze of the audience into an ideal world of transcendent experience beyond self-indulgence and theatrical 'effect' (precisely the faults for which Schreker had been most condemned after *Irrelohe*). It is left to Meister Johann to suggest that a quartet movement, after all, was what was needed: a new kind of chastened music; music redeemed, perhaps, but purified through the fires of bitter experience.

In his subsequently written 'Foreword' to *Christophorus*,[13] Schreker stressed that its message depended upon the parallelism of the role of the child and the creative intimation of "redemption through absolute music", going on to anticipate the question as to why he himself should have written an *opera* about it by implying that that, for better or worse, was what he did best. In conclusion, he suggests that opera itself might be revived and renewed "by reverting to its original character" – Schreker's conception of which produced in *Der Schmied von Gent* a Wunderhorn fantasy, a kind of children's pantomime opera that Gustav Mahler would no doubt have understood far better than those who booed it off the stage in 1932.

★ ★ ★

Terminal figure that he undoubtedly was, Schreker was a remarkable mediator between nineteenth- and twentieth-century conceptions of the nature and purpose of music as an art-form. Looking back to the German Romantic tradition, he succeeded in precariously holding together music and ideas before the former was to retreat into its shell of modern 'objectivity', while the ideas reverted to the sphere of literature whence they had come in the first place. His expression of these ideas may have suffered from his lack of the finesse and judgement of either the true poet or the true philosopher, but they are ideas that strike to the heart of matters that were troubling many creative minds in Europe in the first decades of this century. More important still, they were ideas that were in large measure prompted and generated by his music.

Retaining an unashamed causal connection with the full range of human expression and experience, Schreker's music refused to renounce its right to either the most touching vulnerability, the most elevating beatitude, or the most terrifying destructive

potency of the human soul, ravenous in lust or murderous in hate. Consequently Schreker stands within
the Austro–German tradition as a terminal prac-
titioner of that larger Music which St John
Chrysostom had known in the fourth century A.D. to
be as likely to introduce "harm, ruin, and many grievous matters"[14] into the mind that it might otherwise
uplift. Schreker experienced St John's reservations
about his art-form at first hand and what is remarkable
about his symbolic confrontation of them in his operas
is that it reveals quite clearly that the desire for a
music that might *merely* uplift (if one might so put it)
was patently as much a matter of contemporary
psychopathology as the grievous matters in which it so
readily dealt. And this at a time when the most round-
ed concept of the mind was in essence musical; at a
time when the dynamic fragmentation and complexity
and wantonness of the 'decadent' style in music
matched perfectly the most modern image of man's
inner nature, from which there was every reason to
turn in horror.

All of the major innovatory attempts at 'renewal' in
twentieth-century European music represent in various degrees attempts to curb, to repress, to regiment,
to cut-down-to-size the grand post-Wagnerian manner, be they by Schoenberg, Stravinsky, Satie, Kurt
Weill or whomever. In that they represent something
like the efforts of an ailing culture to preserve its own
Zeitgeist from total derangement, these attempts were
in a way essential. Yet they all rely upon a wilful and
to some extent arbitrary act of self-mastering, even of
self-limitation, which most clearly in Schoenberg pres-

ents the aspect of a pathological kind of asceticism, that logically led his pupil Cage to take a Trappist vow of silence and stop composing altogether.

Schreker had actually long before set the torch to a music that he both loved and feared and, like Cage, had turned to the East for a new source of healing ideas. What *he* chanced upon, however, was not Zen Buddhism or the *I Ching*, but those words of Lao Tzu that come mysteriously out of the darkness that precedes the Epilogue to *Christophorus*. They were abbreviated as follows by Schreker himself in his Foreword to the opera:

> Whoever recognizes his manly strength
> while yet persisting in feminine vulnerability,
> is the river-bed of the world.
> Who knows his light
> while yet tarrying in the darkness
> is the example of the world.
> Who knows his worth
> while yet abiding in dishonour
> is the valley of the world.
> Being the valley of the world
> he will enjoy eternal life
> and can turn again to simplicity.[15]

The 'manly' responses to modern disillusionment included perhaps the humorous evasion, the proudly self-denying dissonance, a hygienic sparseness. But by the late 1920s Schreker had become disillusioned with the facile artistic products of these however-valid responses to a dilemma he well understood. He saw enough of them in the Berlin of that period and wrote in 1929 of the cultural chaos in which he found himself:

Classicism, Romanticism, Impressionism, Expressionism, Late-Romanticism, Constructivism, Neoclassicism, *Neue Sachlichkeit* – in amongst which a little quarter-tone music and imitations of negro music in considerable abundance.... The Berliner finds all this wonderful. Diversity – always something new.... All this following a devastating war. A colourful and most lively period in which our time-honoured musical art is thoroughly tossed about, sieved, refined, coarsened, mutilated, distorted – beaten out of shape in all directions, while from another quarter it is simplified, rolled out and pressed flat.[16]

Suddenly Schreker, the *Neutöner* of the Vienna years, was sounding like Pfitzner, the message of whose *Palestrina* is recast in a fascinating way in the far more modern-looking and modern-sounding *Christophorus*. For do not those words of Lao Tzu suggest that the most complete and perfect satisfaction in life is to be derived from the knowledge and acceptance of the fact that we are none of us either complete or perfect? The fruit of nineteenth-century speculation about the nature of the mind of the 'expressing' artist were ideas which inhibited expression as a communicative act dependent upon a shared language. To accept a new picture of the human mind, in all its contrariety, might well be to accept that the enigmatic dissonance with which *Christophorus* opens is no more nor less a part of the full picture than the vulnerable consolation of the cadential celebration of C major with which the opera closes.

Conclusion

It will have become clear in what way the critical enterprise outlined in these essays relies upon a consideration of ideas about music as much as upon the analytical or musicological study of specific works. While such study must continue to provide the foundation of our detailed knowledge of musical production in any period, it has been proposed that in the cultural context under consideration, in the half-century from about 1890 to the Second World War, composition in the traditionally valued 'high' forms self-consciously incorporated and depended upon ideas to an extent that ignorance or disregard of them must seriously falsify our historical understanding of it. Intellectual attitudes towards the image of the nineteenth-century Artist, towards concepts like inspiration and expressive 'truth', conditioned equally, but in startlingly different ways, the works of all the composers discussed here. In Schoenberg's career they took on an increasingly repressive role, casting doubt upon the continuing value and even the possibility of the art he had inherited, dependent as it had been upon newly devalued notions of the duality of form and content and the expressing individual as a worthy subject.

Proceeding beyond an objective account of these ideas into a more critical examination of them, to the end of demonstrating the questionable logic of the 'inevitability' of their extensive creative consequences, I have broached an explicitly ambivalent evaluation of modernism in European music and explored a renewed interest in other composers and works hitherto consigned to the margins of the musical history of the period. In that they reflect the historical experience that has been the subject-matter of this study, the implications of this approach merit some concluding comment.

My initial questioning of the value of a subjectively determined art-historical approach of the traditional kind, with its series of 'great men' and 'great works', might be recalled here. The central basis for worry is perhaps less our own, late-twentieth-century concern about the so-called relativism of subjective judgements than a recognition of the socially and culturally *determined* aspect of all such judgements. Such recognition jars painfully against the ideal of transcendent, transcultural 'truthfulness' which underpins the modern scientific enterprise that expresses itself, within cultural studies, in anthropology, with its rigorous rejection of ethnocentric premises. To engage in the practice rather than the study of criticism is to enter a hall of mirrors which can be hostile and frightening to the modern intellectual. He looks around and finds his labelled image reflected back and forth into infinity as left-wing, right-wing, conservative, radical, neo-romantic or whatever. Here the self-styled anthropologist, who had sought the throne-room of transcendent understanding, finds himself the despised object of his own study: a creature living within and determined by one culture, one social status and one upbringing. For to be the creature 'of' a culture is to be a puppet, a potential instrument of barbarism or stoker of death-camp ovens as much as neighbour of the great or provider for posterity. Only by constant self-critical vigilance may we avoid the nightmare of History.

Not all commentators would necessarily wish to subscribe to the notion of a purely one-way, causal connection between society and the imaginative life of its participants. But the spectre of a socially determined 'nature' is one that has tormented twentieth-century man – certainly the twentieth-century artist. 'Paint *naturally*, please!', the art-lover cries. 'But nature is what you make it', ponders the harassed artist of radical inclination, and the more one version is reproduced, the more it may condition others to accept the status quo and overlook the repressive arbitrariness of imagined truth. We are back in Adorno's realm of conservative delusion opposed by radical negation, and here it is critics and artists alike who find themselves in the soup.

The alternative, or perhaps compromise path tentatively projected in the foregoing essays would be one that depended upon the requirement to accept both the need to maintain vigilance over the tyranny of our conditioning and the need to 'live' that conditioning if there is to be anything to question or change. Of the composers discussed here, it was perhaps Mahler who most successfully maintained the dual standpoint within his own art of childlike *Einfall* set in the context of an agonizing dialectical form. For this reason he might be considered the presiding genius of the often close-knit group of artists and writers that I have invoked in the attempt to indicate the proper context in which to evaluate the strange and tortuous achievement of Arnold Schoenberg and his numerous progeny amongst European musical modernists. Their quest after transcendent authenticity has consistently born the mark of Schoenberg's own suffering upon the rack of an art that, in becoming the function and illustration of a dominating idea, had renounced its value and even function *as* 'art' in the culturally received meaning of that term. By avoiding the vulnerability of subscribing to an illusion of truth in the subjective expression that depended upon a shared language (and potentially shared misconceptions, therefore), the radical artist achieved his contemporaneity necessarily as a victim rather than an articulator of social truth. By rejecting the bourgeois audience that had created the social possibility of nineteenth-century music, he condemned himself to the role of the uncomprehended outsider, with only ironic counterfeits, mystic invocations and penitential silences with which to beg his keep from those same consumers of art that he had previously rejected.

The extent to which others retained a wide audience and thus an active role within their society, constitutes an essential part of the challenge posed by Strauss,

CONCLUSION

Pfitzner, Schreker and the posthumous Mahler. So too by Thomas Mann, the writer about music and the problems of twentieth-century art who remained the successful purveyor of consumable novels which managed to embody complex ideas about the society in which he lived while offering much to a wide, even popular audience – less for the reason that he pandered to a desire for escapist entertainment than that, with whatever irony at his own expense, he was able to submit to that curious function of what I find myself having once more to describe sociologically as bourgeois art. For all he knew of the dangers and pitfalls and ambivalent power of this art, Mann could not resist practising it in its traditional Western form, which was for him above all a *musical* form, with its "joy in scandalous antireason, its tendency to beauty-creating 'barbarism'": "An irrational power but a great power; and the attachment of people to it proves that people neither can nor want to make do with rationality...."[1] He might have gone on to observe that limited and flawed rationality itself might benefit, rather than suffer, from continued 'indulgent' immersion in its barbarous beauties.

And yet, did not the subsequent experience of the very culture we have been considering contrive a practical admonition of such an attitude? This we are compelled to confront, as Mann was in the two decades following the completion of his *Reflections of a Nonpolitical Man*. The recently exiled musicologist Alfred Einstein confronted it in the pages of the *Musical Times* in November 1933[2], in an article entitled 'The Present State of Music in Germany'. It was his sad duty to record there the first grim stages of the social enforcement of a crude parody of some of the insights of Mann's *Reflections* and Pfitzner's *Futuristengefahr*. Already the "works of 'educational Bolshevist' tendencies, from Mahler to Schoenberg and Alban Berg" were being removed from the repertoire, the new season at the Berlin State Opera relying solely "on Wagner, Verdi, Puccini, and Pfitzner's *Palestrina*." The inevitable politicization of Pfitzner that Mann had half-humorously recorded during the First World War had now been imposed from outside in a newly nightmarish chapter of history. Einstein himself was concerned to stress the tragic injustice of this, observing that Pfitzner's 'Germanness' was of a kind that extended far beyond the narrow definition of the National Socialists. His appeal, Einstein suggests, was of a wholly exclusive kind, sufficiently removed from the vulgarities of mass movements to give one cause to derive "some comfort" from the quotation from Schopenhauer with which Pfitzner had prefaced the score of his opera and whose concluding lines hold that "alongside of the history of the world there goes, guiltless and unstained by blood, the history of philosophy, of science and the arts."[3]

I doubt if we now believe that. Perhaps, indeed, it is *because* we no longer accept the possibility of wholly separating art from society, as we no longer believe in it as an actual or potential repository of transcendent truth, that the quest of Schoenbergian modernism may grow more rather than less problematic with the passing of time. Meanwhile, the music of Pfitzner and Schreker, like that of other once favoured composers of the particular "sunken civilization" we have been considering, is being listened to once more with increasing interest and by an increasingly wide audience. Might not the very extent to which they reveal their guilt and display their bloodstains now encourage us to draw them back into our cultural discourse? The result could be both startling and liberating, although the challenge will be as much to critical as to starved emotional faculties. The ideas that once called into question the latter at the expense of the former can hardly be expected to go away, and the robes of the dispossessed Romantic Artist were long ago sold off to Hollywood.

Notes

Unless otherwise indicated, translations are by the author.

1. Epigraph: *The Works of Friedrich Nietzsche*, Vol. III, Thomas Common (London: T. Fisher Unwin, 1899) p. 72.

CHAPTER ONE

1. See Bruno Walter, *Gustav Mahler*, tr. James Galston, with a biographical essay by Ernst Krenek (New York: Vienna House, 1973), p. 136; and Henry-Louis de La Grange, *Mahler*, Vol. I (London: Gollancz, 1974), pp. 312–13.

2. Albert Goldman and Evert Sprinchorn (eds.), *Wagner on Music and Drama* (New York: E. P. Dutton and Co., 1964), p. 271.

3. *Gustav Mahler, Briefe 1879–1911*, ed. Alma Mahler (Berlin: Paul Zsolnay, 1925), p. 126. See also Knud Martner (ed.), *Selected Letters of Gustav Mahler* (London: Faber and Faber, 1979), p. 412.

4. Bruno Walter (see Note 1), pp. 128–9.

5. Ferdinand Pfohl, *Gustav Mahler, Eindrücke und Erinnerungen aus den Hamburger Jahren*, ed. Knud Martner (Hamburg: Karl Dieter Wagner, 1973), p. 16.

6. Henceforth Will, with a capital 'W', signifies the Schopenhauerian concept.

7. Arthur Schopenhauer, *The World as Will and Representation*, Vol. II, tr. E. J. F. Payne (New York: Dover, 1966), p. 581.

8. I refer here to the text of the second song of the *Lieder eines fahrenden Gesellen* ('Ging heut morgens übers Feld').

9. Alma Mahler, *Gustav Mahler, Memories and Letters*, tr. Basil Creighton, 2nd English ed., ed. Donald Mitchell (London: John Murray, 1968), p. 236.

10. See *Correspondence of Wagner and Liszt*, Vol. II, tr., with a preface by Francis Hueffer, 2nd ed. rev. W. Ashton Ellis (New York: Vienna House, 1973), p. 54.

11. Henry-Louis de La Grange (see Note 1), p. 686.

12. Alma Mahler, *Gustav Mahler, Memories and Letters* (see Note 9), p. 20.

13. The compilation *The Will to Power* had been first published under Nietzsche's name, posthumously, in 1901. That work, and current comment upon it, could well have set the seal on Mahler's disapproval of Nietzsche at this time.

14. See Alma Mahler, *Gustav Mahler, Memories and Letters* (see Note 9), p. 47. I have not been able to trace the source of this 'quotation' from Schopenhauer, and suspect that Alma Mahler merely repeats here Mahler's own slightly garbled version of one of Schopenhauer's passages on noise-makers (he certainly cites whip-cracking as particularly offensive on more than one occasion in *The World as Will and Representation*).

15. Schopenhauer (see Note 7), Vol. II, p. 360.

16. Schopenhauer, op.cit., Vol. I, pp. 184–5.

17. Ibid., p. 186.

18. Ibid., p. 196.
19. Ibid., p. 257.
20. Schopenhauer, op.cit., Vol. II, p. 137.
21. Ibid., p. 138.
22. Ibid., p. 136.
23. Ibid., p. 450.
24. Schopenhauer, op.cit., Vol. I, p. 258.
25. Ibid., p. 259.
26. Schopenhauer, op.cit., Vol. II, p. 129.
27. Alma Mahler, *Gustav Mahler, Memories and Letters* (see Note 9), p. 243.
28. Natalie Bauer-Lechner, *Recollections of Gustav Mahler*, tr. Dika Newlin, ed. and annotated by Peter Franklin (London: Faber Music, 1980), p. 67.
29. Schopenhauer (see Note 7), Vol. I, p. 264.
30. Schopenhauer, op.cit., Vol. II, p. 449.
31. The concepts of both 'Eros' and 'Caritas' are in fact elaborated by Schopenhauer in *The World as Will and Representation*. The Eighth Symphony was originally conceived as a four-movement work whose third and fourth movements were to be entitled *Adagio Caritas* and *Die Geburt des Eros* respectively.
32. Bruno Walter (see Note 1), p. 59.

CHAPTER TWO

1. Otto Klemperer, *Meine Erinnerungen an Gustav Mahler* (Zurich: Atlantis Verlag, 1960), p. 21.
2. Alma Mahler, *Gustav Mahler, Memories and Letters*, tr. Basil Creighton, 2nd English ed., ed. Donald Mitchell (London: John Murray, 1968), p. 98.

3. From Mahler's programme for the Second Symphony (Dresden, 1901), reproduced in Alma Mahler, op. cit., p. 213.

4. The translation is from Henry-Louis de La Grange, *Mahler,* Vol. I (London: Gollancz, 1974), p. 332. See also Knud Martner (ed.), *Selected Letters of Gustav Mahler* (London: Faber and Faber, 1979), p. 160.

5. Norman Del Mar, *Richard Strauss,* Vol. I (London: Barrie and Jenkins, 1962), p. 78.

6. Rolland's diary in *Richard Strauss and Romain Rolland – Correspondence,* ed. and annotated with a preface by Rollo Myers (London: Calder and Boyars, 1968), pp. 111–12.

7. William Mann, *Richard Strauss: a Critical Study of the Operas* (London: Cassell, 1964), p. 167.

8. *Richard Strauss and Romain Rolland – Correspondence* (see Note 6), p. 210.

CHAPTER THREE

1. p. 229. All references are to the Penguin Modern Classics edition of *Doctor Faustus,* tr. H. T. Lowe-Porter (London: Penguin Books, 1968).

2. Thomas Mann, *The Genesis of a Novel,* tr. Richard and Clara Winston (London: Secker & Warburg, 1961), p. 62.

3. Ibid., p. 75.

4. Quoted in Nicolas Slonimsky, *Lexicon of Musical Invective,* 2nd ed. (Seattle and London: University of Washington Press, 1969), p. 150.

5. *The Genesis of a Novel* (see Note 2), p. 75.

6. *Doctor Faustus* (see Note 1), pp. 131–2.

7. Ibid., p. 148.

8. Ibid., p. 148.

9. Ibid., p. 211.
10. Ibid., p. 266.
11. Ibid., p. 25.
12. Ibid., p. 257.
13. Ibid., p. 178.
14. Ibid., p. 471.
15. Ibid., p. 310.
16. Ibid., p. 310.
17. Ibid., p. 393.
18. Ibid., p. 419.
19. Ibid., p. 395.
20. Ibid., p. 236.
21. Thomas Mann, *Essays of Three Decades*, tr. H. T. Lowe-Porter (New York: Knopf, 1976), p. 344.

CHAPTER FOUR

1. Adorno, *Philosophy of Modern Music*, tr. Anne G. Mitchell and Wesley V. Bloomster (London: Sheed and Ward, 1973), p. 13. While the quality of this translation has frequently been questioned – see e.g. Gillian Rose, *The Melancholy Science* (London: Macmillan, 1978), p. 195 – it remains the only one available. The title of the final published version should correctly be rendered 'Philosophy of *New* Music' (*Philosophie der neuen Musik*), see Gillian Rose, op. cit., p. 189 n.225. For textual comparison, the interested reader is referred to the German original: Theodor W. Adorno, *Philosophie der neuen Musik – Gesammelte Schriften, Band 12* (Frankfurt am Main: Suhrkamp, 1975). In the passages quoted, I have included the German where an alternative translation would clearly be possible.

2. Adorno, op. cit., translators' introduction, p. xii. The source is Thomas Mann, *The Genesis of a Novel*, tr. Richard and Clara Winston (London: Secker and Warburg, 1961), pp. 38–9.

3. As Note 2.

4. Adorno, op. cit., p. 39.

5. Ibid., p. 42.

6. See H. H. Stuckenschmidt, *Arnold Schoenberg, his Life, World and Work* (London: John Calder, 1977), p. 508.

7. Adorno (see Note 1), p. 50.

8. Ibid., p. 73.

9. Ibid., p. 67.

10. Ibid., p. 67.

11. Ibid., pp. 67–9.

12. Ibid., p. 68.

13. Ibid., p. 78.

14. Ibid., p. 80.

15. Ibid., p. 82.

16. Ibid., p. 89.

17. Ibid., p. 104.

18. Ibid., p. 69.

19. Ibid., p. 104.

20. Ibid., p. 104.

21. Ibid., p. 104.

22. Ibid., p. 105.

23. Ibid., p. 104.

24. Ibid., p. 105.

25. Ibid., pp. 105–6.

26. Ibid., p. 110.

27. Ibid., p. 109.

28. Ibid., p. 109.

29. Ibid., p. 109.
30. Ibid., p. 109.
31. Ibid., p. 187.
32. Ibid., p. 112.
33. Ibid., p. 116.
34. Ibid., p. 117.
35. Ibid., p. 116.
36. Ibid., p. 114.
37. Ibid., p. 133.
38. Ibid., p. 133.
39. Ibid., p. 132.
40. Ibid., p. 133.
41. Ibid., p. 107.

CHAPTER FIVE

1. Arnold Schoenberg, *Style and Idea*, ed. Leonard Stein, with translations by Leo Black (London: Faber and Faber, 1975), p. 400.
2. Ibid., p. 450.
3. Ibid., p. 453.
4. Ibid., p. 454.
5. Ibid., p. 454.
6. Ibid., p. 463.
7. This statement, omitted without comment in the 1975 edition, will be found in the version of the essay originally published by Dika Newlin – see Arnold Schoenberg, *Style and Idea* (London: Williams and Norgate, 1951), p. 26.
8. *Style and Idea* (1975 ed.), p. 470.
9. Ibid., p. 470.
10. Ibid., p. 470.

11. Ibid., p. 470.

12. Arnold Schoenberg, *Letters,* ed. Erwin Stein (London: Faber and Faber, 1964), p. 243.

13. *Style and Idea* (1975 ed.), p. 449.

14. Ibid., p. 449.

15. The original article which formed the basis of this essay was written on 30 October 1912. (See H. H. Stuckenschmidt, *Arnold Schoenberg, his Life, World and Work* (London: John Calder, 1977), p. 108.

16. *Style and Idea* (1975 ed.), p. 449.

17. Ibid., p. 449.

18. Ibid., p. 449.

19. Ibid., p. 450.

20. Ibid., p. 452.

21. Ibid., p. 452.

22. Ibid., p. 452.

23. Ibid., p. 457.

24. Ibid., p. 457.

25. Ibid., p. 458.

26. Ibid., p. 459.

27. Ibid., p. 463.

28. Ibid., p. 464.

29. Ibid., p. 468.

30. Ibid., p. 470.

31. Ibid., p. 471.

32. Ibid., p. 471.

CHAPTER SIX

1. Joseph Rufer, *The Works of Arnold Schoenberg. A Catalogue,* tr. Dika Newlin (London: Faber and Faber, 1962), Appendix to 'Theoretical Works'

(p. 140), No. 4. See also Arnold Schoenberg, *Letters,* ed. Erwin Stein (London: Faber and Faber, 1964), p. 164.

2. Joseph Rufer, op. cit., No. 9.

3. See the leaflet provided with the CBS recording *The Music of Arnold Schoenberg,* Vol. 2 (BRG 72268), 1965.

4. Arnold Schoenberg, *Style and Idea,* ed. Leonard Stein, with translations by Leo Black (London: Faber and Faber, 1975), p. 237.

5. Schoenberg, *Letters* (see Note 1), p. 243.

6. Theodor Adorno, *Philosophy of Modern Music,* tr. Anne G. Mitchell and Wesley V. Bloomster (London: Sheed and Ward, 1973), p. 39.

7. See ibid., p. 89.

8. Nietzsche, *The Birth of Tragedy* (with *The Case of Wagner*), ed. Walter Kaufmann (New York: Vintage Books, 1967), p. 60.

9. My translation.

10. H. H. Stuckenschmidt, *Arnold Schoenberg, his Life, World and Work* (London: John Calder, 1977), p. 205.

11. See above, Ch. 5, p. 81.

12. See Note 3 above.

13. Schoenberg, *Style and Idea* (see Note 4), p. 457.

14. *Moses und Aron,* I. iv.

15. Ibid., II. v.

16. Ibid., conclusion of Act II.

17. John Cage, *Silence* (Cambridge, Mass. and London: The M.I.T. Press, 1966), p. 154.

18. Ibid., p. 195.

19. Ibid., p. 195.

20. Jonathan Cott, *Stockhausen: Conversations with the Composer* (London: Pan Books, 1974), p. 150.

21. Pierre Boulez, *Conversations with Celestin Deliège* (London: Eulenburg, 1976), p. 56.

22. Ibid., pp. 56–7.

23. Taken from the booklet accompanying the Bärenreiter *Musicaphon* recording (*New Music from Basle*, BM 30 SL 1715).

CHAPTER SEVEN

1. This work, first published in Berlin in 1919, is now available in English as *Reflections of a Nonpolitical Man*, tr., with an introduction, by Walter D. Morris (New York: Frederick Ungar, 1983). The relevant section is the latter part of Chapter 8 ('On Virtue'), pp. 297–314. The translations of the extracts quoted here are mostly by Jon Newsom, whose article (see Note 2 below) first drew my attention to this formerly somewhat inaccessible work of Mann's.

2. Jon Newsom, 'Hans Pfitzner, Thomas Mann and *The Magic Mountain*', *Music and Letters*, Vol. 55/2, April 1974, p. 141.

3. Ibid., p. 142.

4. Ibid., p. 141.

5. Max Graf, *Die Wiener Oper* (Vienna: Humbolt–Verlag, 1955), p. 311.

6. Jon Newsom (see Note 2), p. 140.

7. Ibid., p. 141.

8. See above, p. 73.

9. Alma Mahler–Werfel, *And the Bridge is Love* (London: Hutchinson, 1959), p. 30.

10. Ibid., p. 193.

11. See Mosco Carner, 'Pfitzner *v.* Berg or Inspiration *v.* Analysis': *The Musical Times*, May 1977, p. 379.

12. The translation from which quotations have been taken appears in *Three Classics in the Aesthetics of Music* (New York: Dover, 1962), but is of one of the earlier versions of the essay. The material of the final version is somewhat rearranged.

13. See H. H. Stuckenschmidt, *Arnold Schoenberg, his Life, World and Work* (London: John Calder, 1977), pp. 224–5.

14. Ferruccio Busoni, *Sketch of a New Aesthetic of Music* (see Note 12), p. 77.

15. Hans Pfitzner, *Futuristengefahr (Bei Gelegenheit von Busonis Ästhetik)*, *Süddeutsche Monatshefte* (Leipzig-Munich, 1917), p. 4.

16. Ferruccio Busoni, *'The Essence of Music' and other papers*, tr. Rosamond Ley (London: Rockliff, 1957), p. 19.

17. Hans Pfitzner (see Note 15), pp. 14–15.

18. Ibid., p. 13.

19. Ibid., p. 13.

20. Ibid., pp. 17–18.

21. Ibid., p. 42.

22. Ibid., p. 44.

23. Ibid., p. 45.

24. Ibid., pp. 45–6.

25. Ibid., p. 47.

26. Ibid., pp. 47–8.

27. Ibid., p. 48.

28. Jon Newsom (see Note 2), p. 141.

29. *The New Grove Dictionary of Music* (London: Macmillan, 1980). From the Pfitzner article by Helmut Wirth, Vol. 14, p. 613.

30. See Jon Newsom (Note 2), p. 142. Mann, in his *Reflections of a Nonpolitical Man* (see Note 1) had registered the fact that Pfitzner became outwardly

'politicized' during the course of the First World War, longing for military triumph for Germany and even dedicating the op.27 Violin Sonata to Fleet Admiral von Tirpitz "while the surge of submarine warfare was at its height" (pp. 312–13).

31. Quotations from the libretto of *Palestrina* are all taken from the translation by Veronica Slater accompanying the 1973 Deutsche Grammophon recording.

32. Hans Pfitzner (see Note 15), p. 18.

33. Bruno Walter, *Theme and Variations*, tr. James Galston (London: Hamish Hamilton, 1947), p. 247.

34. Thomas Mann, *Reflections of a Nonpolitical Man* (see Note 1), p. 297.

CHAPTER EIGHT

1. J.-K. Huysmans, *Against Nature*, tr. Robert Baldick (London: Penguin Books, 1979), p. 183.

2. Oscar Wilde, *The Picture of Dorian Gray* (from the conclusion of Chapter 10).

3. Huysmans (see Note 1), p. 96.

4. Ibid., p. 204.

5. Ibid., p. 63.

6. Alma Mahler-Werfel, *And the Bridge is Love* (London: Hutchinson, 1959), p. 68.

7. Quoted by H. Schreker-Bures in 'Franz Schreker und seine Zeit', included in Schreker-Bures, Stuckenschmidt and Oehlmann, *Franz Schreker* (Österreichischer Komponisten des XX Jahrhunderts – Band 17, Vienna: Elisabeth Lafite & Österreichischer Bundesverlag, 1970), p. 22.

8. In 1933. See essay by H. H. Stuckenschmidt in Schreker-Bures, Stuckenschmidt and Oehlmann op. cit., p. 44.

9. Ibid., p. 47.

10. See ibid., p. 20.

11. See Christopher Hailey, 'Zur Entstehungs-geschichte der Oper *Christophorus*', included in Elmar Budde and Rudolph Stephan (eds.), *Franz-Schreker-Symposion* (Berlin: Colloquium Verlag, 1980), p. 117.

12. Schreker-Bures etc. (see Note 7), p. 35.

13. See Christopher Hailey (see Note 11), pp. 136–7.

14. Oliver Strunk, *Source Readings in Music History* (London: Faber and Faber, 1981), Vol. I, p. 68.

15. See Christopher Hailey (see Note 11), p. 137. The lines come from Section 28 of the *Tao Te Ching* by Lao Tzu ('Laotse' in German usage). The problem of translation is considerable, as witness the number of modern English translations of the *Tao Te Ching*. I have here attempted to translate the German version used by Schreker in his libretto (from Richard Wilhelm's 1911 translation).

16. Schreker-Bures etc. (see Note 7), pp. 30–31.

CONCLUSION

1. Thomas Mann, *Reflections of a Nonpolitical Man,* tr., with an introduction by Walter D. Morris (New York: Frederick Ungar, 1983), p. 289.

2. I am grateful to Valentine Schmidt for drawing my attention to this article in the *Musical Times* of November 1933, pp. 977–9.

3. The translation is Hans Keller's, from his article 'Schopenhauer's *Palestrina*' in *The Listener*, 23 May 1968, p. 676.

Index

Adorno, Theodor
Wiesengrund, 58–9, 91, 92
——, *Philosophie der neuen Musik (Philosophy of Modern Music)*, 36, 48, 52, 55–75, 90, 94–5, 118–19, 120, 123, 130–31, 134, 163, 173n. 1

Bach, Johann Sebastian, 101–2, 129
Bartók, Béla, 36, 103
Baudelaire, Charles, 141
Bauer–Lechner, Natalie, 14
Beardsley, Aubrey, 142
Beethoven, Ludwig van, xii, 11, 13, 21, 24, 26, 49, 58, 68, 81, 129
——, Symphony no. 9, 53
Bekker, Paul, 147
Berg, Alban, xiii, 59, 70, 91, 124, 144, 148, 166
——, *Wozzeck*, 148

Berio, Luciano, 37
Berliner, Arnold, 1, 2
Berlioz, Hector, 141
Boulez, Pierre, xiii, 112
——, *Structures*, 112
Brahms, Johannes, xii, 78
Busoni, Ferruccio, 124
——, *Entwurf einer neuen Aesthetik der Tonkunst (Sketch of a New Aesthetic of Music)*, 125–30, 179n.12

Cage, John, 37, 109–10, 159
Cahill, Thaddeus, 129
Chaplin, Charlie, *Modern Times*, 100
Craft, Robert, 103

Davies, Peter Maxwell, 37
Debussy, Claude, 42, 141, 142
Deliège, Célestin, 112

INDEX

Del Mar, Norman, 24
Dostoyevsky, Fyodor, 5

Einstein, Alfred, 165–66

Ferneyhough, Brian, 113
——, *Time and Motion
Study II*, 113–14
Freud, Sigmund, 4, 10, 15,
27, 43, 50, 53, 94, 96, 143,
148
——, *Die Traumdeutung
(The Interpretation of
Dreams)*, 95

Gerhard, Roberto, 103–5,
109
Goethe, Johann Wolfgang
von, 21
——, *Faust*, 3, 27, 48
Goncourt, Edmond de, 139,
140
Graf, Max, 121

Hauptmann, Gerhardt, 145
Hegel, Georg W. F., 60
Hoffmann, E. T. A., 25, 148
Hofmannsthal, Hugo von,
22, 30
Horkheimer, Max, 59
Hummel, Johann
Nepomuk, xii
Huysmans, Joris-Karl,
140–41, 142
——, *À Rebours (Against
Nature)*, 139–43, 144, 145

I Ching, 109, 159

Janáček, Leoš, 138

Kandinsky, Wassily, 94, 95
Kant, Immanuel, 3, 42
Keller, Hans, xii
Klemperer, Otto, 19, 21, 22
Klimt, Gustav, 98, 145
Kolisch, Rudolf, 91
Krauss, Clemens, 124
Kunstschau (Vienna 1908),
145

Lang, Fritz, *Metropolis*, 100
Lao Tzu (Laotse), *Tao Te
Ching*, 159, 160, 181n.5
Leavis, F. R., xiv
Leichtentritt, Hugo, 39
Ligeti, György, 36
Luther, Martin, 47
Lutosławski, Witold, 36

Maeterlinck, Maurice, 6
Mahler, Alma, 1, 6, 7, 13,
124, 144–45, 170n.14
Mahler, Gustav, xiv, 1–3,
5–7, 12–17, 19, 21–6, 27,
31, 33, 34, 53, 58, 62, 64,
79–90, 98, 101, 102,
145–6, 157, 164, 166,
170nn. 13 & 14
——, *Lieder eines fahrenden
Gesellen*, 5
——, *Das Lied von der Erde*,
16, 17

——, Symphony no. 1, 17, 23, 24

——, Symphony no. 2, 6, 14, 21–24

——, Symphony no. 3, 1, 3, 13, 14, 16

——, Symphony no. 5, 13

——, Symphony no. 6, 13, 14, 81, 86, 89

——, Symphony no. 7, 15, 124

——, Symphony no. 8, 15, 16, 27, 134, 171n.31

——, Symphony no. 9, 81, 89

——, Symphony no. 10, 81, 89, 90, 103, 107

——, Todtenfeier, 22

Mallarmé, Stéphane, 140, 141

——, L'Après-midi d'un faune, 141

Mann, Thomas, 57, 58–9, 119, 122–23, 131, 132–33, 138, 140–41, 145, 146, 165–66

——, Doctor Faustus, 35–53, 56, 89, 120, 123, 145

——, The Magic Mountain (Der Zauberberg), 119–20, 123

——, Reflections of a Non-political Man (Betrach-tungen eines Unpolitischen), 119–20, 122, 165–6, 178n. 1, 179n. 30

——, 'Sufferings and Greatness of Richard Wagner' ('Leiden und Grösse Richard Wagners'), 50–51

Marc, Maria, 98, 99

Marx, Karl, 140

Messiaen, Olivier, Mode de valeurs et d'intensités, 112

Moreau, Gustave, 143

Mozart, Wolfgang Amadeus, 25, 32

Musical Times, 165–66

Newlin, Dika, 79, 175n.7

Newsom, John, 178n.1

Nietzsche, Friedrich, 6, 7, 22, 25, 26, 27, 31, 36, 43, 46, 50, 96, 125, 144, 146, 147, 170n.13

——, Thus spoke Zarathustra (Also sprach Zarathustra), 34

——, The Will to Power (Der Wille zur Macht), 170n.13

Obukhov, Nikolay, 118

Palestrina, Giovanni Pierluigi da, Missa Papae Marcelli, 121, 134

Pappenheim, Marie, 96

Penderecki, Krzysztof, 36

Pfitzner, Hans, 117–38, 160, 164, 166, 179–80n.30

——, Danger of the Futurists

INDEX

(*Futuristengefahr*), 126–31, 134–35, 138, 166
——, *Palestrina*, 117, 119, 120–38, 160, 166
——, Violin Sonata op.27, 180n.30
Pfohl, Ferdinand, 2
Plato, 4
Poe, Edgar Allan, 141
Puccini, Giacomo, 85, 166
——, *Turandot*, 27

Rolland, Romain, 26–7, 31
Rose, Gillian, 173n.1

St John Chrysostom, 158
Satie, Erik, 158
Schenker, Heinrich, xii
Schiele, Egon, 98
Schindler, Alma, *see* Mahler, Alma
Schoenberg, Arnold, xiii, 20, 25, 29, 32, 36, 37, 39, 40, 53, 56, 57, 58, 63–75, 77–90, 91–115, 118–19, 120, 124, 125, 131, 141, 142, 143, 144, 153, 158–59, 161, 164, 166
——, 'Brahms the Progressive', 78
——, *Das Buch der hängenden Gärten* op. 15, 97
——, *Erwartung*, 29, 53, 60, 63, 65, 66, 95–7, 99
——, Five Orchestral Pieces op. 16, 39, 63, 95, 99
——, *Gurrelieder*, 142
——, 'Gustav Mahler', 79–90, 105, 176n.15
——, *Die glückliche Hand*, 98, 99
——, *Harmonielehre*, 77
——, *Moses und Aron*, 84, 106–7, 129
——, *Pelleas und Melisande*, 29, 142
——, *Pierrot Lunaire*, 98
——, String Quartet no. 2, 97, 98
——, *Style and Idea*, 79, 92, 175n.7
——, Three Piano Pieces op.11, 97, 99
——, Variations for Orchestra op. 31, 92, 100–106
——, Wind Quintet op. 26, 57
Schopenhauer, Arthur, 1–17, 27, 86–7, 147, 166, 170n.14, 171n.31
——, *The World as Will and Representation (Die Welt als Wille und Vorstellung)*, 2–17, 170n.14, 171n.31
Schreker, Franz, 142–60, 164, 166
——, *Christophorus*, 153–57, 159, 160
——, *Der ferne Klang*, 146, 148–49

INDEX

——, *Der Geburtstag der Infantin*, 145
——, *Die Gezeichneten*, 142–43, 144, 145, 146–47
——, *Irrelohe*, 151–52, 153, 156
——, *Der Schatzgräber*, 151
——, *Der Schmied von Gent*, 153, 157
——, *Der singende Teufel*, 152, 154
——, *Das Spielwerk und die Prinzessin*, 149–51
Shakespeare, William, *Hamlet*, 96
Shostakovich, Dmitri, 132
Sibelius, Jean, 138, 164
Skryabin, Alexander, *Mysterium*, 118
Sophocles, 28
Stein, Erwin, 92
Steuermann, Eduard, 59
Stockhausen, Karlheinz, 111
——, *Mantra*, 111–12
Strauss, Richard, xiv, 19–34, 53, 124, 164
——, *Eine Alpensinfonie*, 29
——, *Also sprach Zarathustra*, 34
——, *Arabella*, 33
——, *Ariadne auf Naxos*, 29, 30
——, *Don Juan*, 34
——, *Elektra*, xiv, 27–8, 29, 30 32–3
——, *Ein Heldenleben*, 34

——, *Intermezzo*, 33
——, *Der Rosenkavalier*, 29, 30, 31, 32, 33, 121
——, *Salome*, 27, 29
——, *Sinfonia Domestica*, 31, 34
——, *Till Eulenspiegel*, 34 ,
——, *Tod und Verklärung*, 21–4, 29
——, *Vier letzte Lieder*, 26
Stravinsky, Igor, xiii, 32, 36, 53, 57–8, 66, 71, 142, 158
Strindberg, August, 145

Tchaikovsky, Piotr Il'yich, xii, 32, 83, 93
——, *Romeo and Juliet*, 24
Tirpitz, Fleet Admiral von, 180n.30

Verdi, Giuseppe, 166
Verlaine, Paul, 140, 141

Wagner, Richard, 1, 2, 3, 6, 13, 21, 24, 25, 26, 30, 43–4, 46, 49, 50, 64, 66, 98, 125, 129, 141, 146, 147, 166,
——, *Beethoven*, 2
——, *Die Meistersinger*, 43, 51, 122
——, *Tristan und Isolde*, 6, 63–4
——, *Parsifal*, 121, 144
——, *Die Walküre*, 27–8
Walker, Alan, xii

INDEX

Walter, Bruno, 1, 2, 17, 138
Webern, Anton, xiii, 65, 70, 91, 144
Weill, Kurt, 158

Wilde, Oscar, 145
Wilhelm II, Kaiser, 26
Wilhelm, Richard, 181n.15
Wordsworth, William, 43